THE SCHOOL AIDES SERIES

Series Editor: Joseph Chapel
Director of the Reading Center
Western Michigan University

Titles in the Series Include:

R. Erickson and E. Erickson - **CHILDREN WITH READING PROBLEMS: A GUIDEBOOK FOR PARENTS**

R. Rogers, E. Erickson and R. B. Park - **THE READING TUTOR'S HANDBOOK: GRADES 2-6**

READING ASSESSMENT BOOKLET: GRADES 2-6

STUDENT'S READING TEST BOOK: GRADES 2-6

M. Veele - **THE SCHOOL VOLUNTEER'S HANDBOOK**

Titles in Preparation Include:
(available February, 1978)

THE READING TUTOR'S HANDBOOK: GRADES 7-12

THE READING TUTOR'S HANDBOOK: For Visually Impaired Students

THE READING TUTOR'S HANDBOOK: For Hearing Impaired Students

THE READING TUTOR'S HANDBOOK:
GRADES 2-6

Ruth Evelyn Rogers, M.A.
Edsel L. Erickson, Ed.D.
Ruth Burkett Park, M.S.

LEARNING PUBLICATIONS INC.
Box 1326
Holmes Beach, Florida 33509

Learning Publications, Inc.
P. O. Box 1326
Holmes Beach, Florida 33509

Designed by Darryl Pfau

Library of Congress Catalog Card Number 77-1247

Hardback: ISBN 0-918452-00-7
Paperback: ISBN 0-918452-01-5

Printing: 1 2 3 4 5 6 7 8   Year: 7 8 9 0 1

Printed in the United States of America

Dedicated

to

Our Teachers and Students

ACKNOWLEDGEMENTS

Our thanks must go to many persons. This book benefits from having its materials tested by many college student tutors and lay persons. We are grateful for their constructive feedback. We also appreciate being able to adapt materials from our earlier book *How to Diagnose and Correct Your Child's Reading Problem* published by Teaching and Learning Publications, Inc.

For suggestions, comments and criticisms of the manuscript, we wish to express gratitude to Joseph Chapel, our consulting editor and Director of the Reading Clinic, Western Michigan University, William Holladay, Associate Editor of *Reading Horizons*, and Lee M. Joiner, Professor of Education, Southern Illinois University. We are also very appreciative of Barbara McFadden's editorial and production assistance, patience and staunch support.

We also wish to express our thanks to the many educators who have been our colleagues and our students who have made ours an exciting and good profession.

CONTENTS

PART A

INTRODUCTION TO TUTORING

1

Your Objectives

Students who have been singled out for tutoring in reading, although they differ in other ways, have one characteristic in common: they have difficulty in reading, an area of learning that is basic to school performance—and to life in general.

ADVANTAGES OF TUTORING

As a tutor, you will find yourself in a role that is both unique and advantageous. You will find that tutoring enables you to form relationships with students that differ from those of their teachers and parents. By working on a one-to-one basis, with professional support and guidance, you can develop and conduct an individually-focused program for each student. You will be able to help students improve their reading skills.

This book describes how you can be a successful reading tutor. It explains how you may assess each student's specific reading difficulties. In addition, it describes what you can do to overcome individual reading problems—a job that cannot be done unless you have each student's cooperation.

BUILDING TRUST

Among your first tasks is to get acquainted with each of the persons you are to tutor in such a way that he or she will regard you as a friend—not merely as a teacher-helper, or as a parent-substitute for supervision of homework—but as someone who will provide special help and attention; who cares; who tries to understand in order to be of help.

SHARING GOALS

In addition to trusting you, your students must come to share your goal of overcoming their reading deficiencies. As they grow to accept that goal and work for it willingly, your students will become aware that: 1) the act of reading can be pleasurable and interesting; 2) good reading skills can help them in attaining other goals; and 3) by co-operating with you, they can become better readers.

At the beginning, improvement in performance will be the main goal. However, as your students progress they will gradually realize that *the act of reading has something in it for them*; that knowing how to read not only "pays off" in school but brings enrichment to their existence, in ways they may have never before imagined.

With the help of this book and its accompanying materials, you can tutor each student to better reading performance and in addition, you can lead most students to new appreciation for the printed word and its significance in their lives.

SUPPLEMENTARY RESOURCES

This handbook and its supplementary materials, the *Reading Assessment Booklet: Grades 2-6*, and the *Student's Reading Test Book: Grades 2-6*, provide tests and examination procedures which can be used to assess typical difficulties and measure improvements in reading skills.

If professional diagnostic testing has already been done, you will still find the tests in these materials to be of great help in establishing rapport on the first day. More importantly, these tests will help you to understand why a student's teacher or parent has asked for tutoring service. You will gain insight into the problems you are being asked to help resolve.

In addition to techniques for helping you zero in on each student's own special reading problems, exercises for the development of needed skills are given in this handbook. Even on the first day you will be able to demonstrate that you can help a student to read better. In Part D we will discuss methods for providing immediate results.

Of course, fundamental changes in reading skills will take more time; but students who recognize some improvement with each succeeding session will tend to devote that time willingly.

THE IMPORTANCE OF PROGRESS

A sense of progress is a great facilitator of further success, while discouragement causes a sense of futility and failure. The activities and tests presented in this handbook and its supplementary materials will help you demonstrate reading growth to your students, their teachers and their parents.

Real proof of progress, however, will be reflected in each student's school performance. The majority of individuals who receive a well-planned and executed tutorial program, which is coordinated with the efforts of their teachers, will also show improvement in the classroom. Furthermore, students who begin to read better will automatically show improvement in their other school subjects. When school achievement is enhanced, so is pleasure in school; and of course, pleasure and success in school can make a better life possible.

You have the opportunity to make a major contribution to the life of each student you tutor.

2

Protocol And Ethics

To be successful, tutoring requires a firm, reliable commitment to give of your time for a specific period of time. As stated in the directions of one university-sponsored tutorial service, "A program that starts and flourishes and then stops suddenly is an unsuccessful program. The community [including students, parents and teachers] needs to feel assured that it will not be abandoned . . . and also that your tutor service is not just a whim."*

YOUR COMMITMENTS

Tutoring that is not carried out as planned may not only be disruptive to a student, but may be disruptive to an entire program of activities. Teachers must plan for when a student is to be taken from a room. They must coordinate many activities. Accordingly, by honoring your

---

Pegasus Tutor's Program Booklet, Kalamazoo, Michigan, Department of Directed Teaching, School of Education, Western Michigan University, 1976, p. 2.

agreement to tutor at scheduled times, you will be carrying out your part of an ethical arrangement.

EMERGENCIES

Of course, certain unforeseen personal emergencies
may come up. Should a situation arise which makes you
late or unable to keep an appointment, telephone your
supervisor or the teacher as early as possible and offer a
new arrangement for meeting the student (or cancel the
session). If you carry the school's phone number with you
at all times, this will enable you to easily telephone or send
word in cases of emergency, and your courtesy will be
appreciated.

CHECK IN AT THE OFFICE

On your first entrance to a school building, and on
each succeeding day that you enter, *be sure* to check in at
the office. Building administrators need to know that you
are on the premises and why you are there. Unless you
have been specifically directed otherwise, your failure to
announce yourself at each visit will be considered by most
principals to be a gross discourtesy. Whether or not the
principal is in, notify the office secretary why you are
there and the names of persons you have arranged to meet.

If you are taking part in a volunteer program that is being directly supervised by a staff member (probably a teacher), it may not be necessary for you to stop at the office each time you enter the building. Your supervisor should provide you with guidelines for courteous and professional conduct in carrying out your duties; if this is not done, and if you are not familiar with school protocol, ask for the information.

DRESS

Dress neatly in clothing that is consitent with the norms of the school. Your attire should reflect your professional commitments to be of service to students; consequently, your appearance should attract no undue attention but should exemplify standards in effect at the school.

HEALTH

Health matters are of particular interest to schools, for obvious reasons. If you get a reasonable amount of rest each night, you can maintain cheerfulness and efficiency while keeping yourself less susceptible to illness.

When illness cannot be avoided, *never* try to keep up your duties in spite of it; you will accomplish more in the long run if you allow yourself time to recuperate. A more important reason for staying away from the school during illness is the risk of spreading contagious disease—which can present a real threat to the school's total program.

Most schools require that all employees, including tutors, submit to tuberculosis tests. This is usually a routine procedure but if you are not asked to get a patch test, inquire about it. You should be checked for TB before working with youngsters.

TAKING STUDENTS FROM CLASSROOMS

The importance of meeting commitments has been mentioned, and punctuality is one of the primary factors to be considered. When you are scheduled to see a student at an appointed time, arrive precisely at that time—not early and not late. Bear in mind that the teacher strives to achieve a smooth running classroom program; your tutoring must fit into that program. By the same token, return the student to the classroom at the agreed-upon time—not early and not late.

Under no circumstances should you leave a student alone or allow a student to return unsupervised to the classroom. During the period set aside for tutoring, you are responsible for the student; so, depending on the age and reliability of each student, make necessary supervision even during breaks for a drink of water or a bathroom visit. Such supervision need not be oppressive to the student; in fact, it can be extremely casual; just remember *you are in charge*, so it is best to make sure you know what the student is doing until placed under the supervision of a regular member of the school staff.

EMERGENCIES

Do not wait for an emergency situation to arise before learning what must be done. Most schools have plans for various emergencies. Find out what you are to do in case a student becomes ill, runs away or becomes an uncontrollable disciplinary problem. In addition, find out in advance about all types of building alarms for other emergencies. In particular, be prepared to follow the rules for fire and disaster drills. In any event, stay with your student until you are relieved by a school staff member.

PROFESSIONAL INTEGRITY

Doctors, teachers, lawyers and other professionals make it a practice to respect the privacy of clients. The problems, characteristics and confidences of your students and their parents should never be discussed with anyone who does not have a professional right or need to know them. If you avoid gossip about students, parents and

school personnel, your professional status will be enhanced. You may also save your client and yourself from possible embarrassment or even serious trouble.

To uphold professional integrity, however, it is your
duty to report all relevant observations and concerns to
those in authority. If you find out something about a student which your supervisor or the school principal should
know in order to help that student, by all means report it
to the appropriate authcrity. Also, if you have difficulty in
following plans for successful tutoring of any student, discuss the matter with your supervisor promptly. Trying to
correct the situation yourself may merely make it worse.

There is a great deal of talent in every school, available for consultation in just such circumstances; and no-
body will expect you to achieve perfect results all the
time. After checking with your supervisor (if he or she is
not the student's teacher), you may wish to consult with
the teacher or a reading specialist and share your tutoring
problems. Do not be afraid to share your difficulties and
uncertainties with others who may be able to come to
your aid.

It goes without saying that any health problems you
may notice in a student should be reported to your supervisor who will in turn refer the matter to the school nurse.
Similarly, if you are convinced that a physical examination, a hearing or visual test or a psychological evaluation
might help to pinpoint a student's deficiencies, offer these
observations to your advisor.

PREPARATION IS IMPORTANT

In a later section we will detail materials which you should have with you. If you finish your planned activities early, be prepared with additional activities. After a tutoring session, plan the next session as soon as possible and give a copy of the plan to your supervisor.

STUDENT RECORDS AND PRIVACY

Most states have laws that do not allow anyone except parents and authorized school staff to examine student records. Of course, school teachers and reading specialists have access to such records. If it is deemed to be in a student's interest and you are working under school supervision, relevant information can be provided to you upon request.

In any event, obtain student records information only through your supervisor, and *do not* release this information to any unauthorized person. If you release personal data on students to unauthorized persons, you may be subject to a law suit.

Remember, the reason for maintaining the confidentiality of records is for humanitarian as well as for professional reasons. The following *Code of Ethics for Tutors* is presented to highlight the humanitarian and professional contributions you may make and enjoy as a tutor:

CODE OF ETHICS FOR TUTORS*

As a tutor, volunteer or paid, I realize that I am subject to a code of ethics similar to that which binds the professionals in the field in which I work. Like them, I assume certain responsibilities and expect to account for what I do in terms of what I am expected to do. I will keep confidential matters confidential. I interpret "volunteer" to mean that I have agreed to work without compensation in money, but having been accepted as a worker, I expect to do my work according to standards, as the paid staff expect to do their work.

I promise to take to my work an attitude of open-mindedness, to be willing to be trained for it; to bring to it interest and attention. I realize that I may have assets that my co-workers may not have and that I should use these to enrich the students for whom we are working together. I realize also that I may lack assets that my co-workers have, but I will not let this make me feel inadequate but will endeavor to assist in developing good teamwork.

I plan to find out how I can best serve the students I will tutor and to offer as much as I am sure I can give, but no more. I realize that I must live up to my promises and

---

*Adapted from "Code of Ethics for Volunteers," *Pegasus Tutor's Program Booklet*, Ibid., p. 4.

therefore, will be careful that my agreement is so simple and clear that it cannot be misunderstood.

I believe that my attitude toward tutoring should be professional. I believe that I have an obligation to my work, to those who direct it, to my colleagues, to those for whom it is done and to the public.

Being eager to contribute all that I can to human betterment, I accept this code for tutors as my code to be followed.

3

Teacher Conferences

Your first conference with the teacher of a student you are to tutor should not be held on the day of your first tutorial session. An introductory time with the student's teacher beforehand—usually twenty to thirty minutes—to acquaint yourselves with each other and to review your competencies and interests is of the utmost importance.

The teacher will need time to plan coordinated activities for you and the student. Additionally, you will need some time to learn about each student with whom you will be working and the teacher's evaluations of his or her problems and capabilities.

THE TEACHER IS RESPONSIBLE

Remember, the teacher is the one who is directly responsible for instruction in school; as a tutor, you will be providing a very important service which is essentially supplementary and complementary to the teacher's role. Your task is not to supplant the teacher, or even to offer unsolicited suggestions concerning teaching procedures.

QUESTIONS TO ASK

In the previous chapter we suggested several questions to ask regarding your role in the school. The first meeting with your student's teacher is the time to ask all questions concerning school protocol that are in need of clarification.

Any additional information you can acquire about procedures to be followed with particular students will assist you in tutoring. Furthermore, knowing about students beforehand can help you establish appropriate relations with staff members as well as students.

Almost any teacher will appreciate amicable support and cooperation in improving a student's reading skills. The teacher will usually be pleased to answer any questions you may have—especially those that draw upon his or her particular experience and insights.

Following is a suggested list of mutual-interest questions* you might ask a teacher. The list is by no means complete for each student you may tutor, however, these can help you get started.

---

*Adapted by permission from *School Data Form*, Reading Center and Clinic, Western Michigan University, 1976, pp. 2-3.

1. At what instructional level is this student reading?

2. Is this student aware that he or she has a reading problem? If so, do you think this student wishes to improve and is willing to put forth effort to do so?

3. What is this student's attitude toward reading?

4. What kind of a reading program has this student experienced in the past?

5. What kind of a reading program is this student in now?

6. Have you ever given this pupil special attention in relation to his or her reading difficulty? What was the nature of this attention?

7. Did this student seem to realize that he or she needed help?

8. Do you think that you have this student's confidence? If so, what problems does he or she discuss with you?

9. How well adjusted is this student in the classroom?

10. Does this student get along well with other children?

11. Do any of this student's peers make any exceptionally commendable remarks about him or her? If so, what kind are they?

12. What has this student been successful in doing?

13. What are this student's extra-curricular activities?

14. What is this student's attitude toward you? Does he or she seem to like you and want to please you or is he or she defiant and disobedient?

15. How regular is this pupil's attendance?

16. Is this pupil shy, quiet, self-conscious, introverted, easily offended?

17. Is this student cheerful, humorous, distractible, depressed, indifferent, cooperative?

18. Does this student show self-confidence?

19. Does this pupil require any special disciplinary measures? If so, can you describe?

20. Has this pupil ever shown any unusual aptitude or interest in any one subject?

21. Is this student able to keep at a task until finished or is he or she easily distracted?

22. Can this pupil follow directions, work independently, and assume responsibility or does he or she require individual help?

23. What can you say of the quality of work which he or she is doing in school?

24. As far as you know, is this pupil suffering from any physical disorder or abnormality of any kind? If so, state what it is.

25. What do you think is the probable cause or causes of this pupil's difficulty?

As was stated previously, in most school systems access to the official records of students is limited to the professional staff and parents. However, if you are working in a school building as part of some authorized school program, all necessary available information will probably be provided to you.

CONFIDENTIAL MATTERS

It must be re-emphasized that any information given you from school records or by school personnel should be held in strict confidence and released to only those who are by law entitled to such information. As pointed out in Chapter 2, just as physicians, teachers and lawyers do not discuss their clients with others except in appropriate professional situations, you too must respect the integrity of the students, their parents and the school staff. Impropriety in this regard could have serious consequences for both you and the student.

4

Meeting Students

Most problem readers face a tutor for the first time with apprehension. Your students are likely to have had many difficult experiences with reading—possibly including school failure and/or failure to improve with special help. This is sure to affect their attitudes toward you.

Students react to failure in various ways, depending on their personality and individual defense mechanisms against painful experiences. Your first contacts may involve students who appear hostile, or indifferent, or withdrawn or subtly determined to frustrate you. Every student you meet, however, will be suffering from some apprehension about meeting you and watching for clues as to your attitudes. A key to your success will be your ability to put each student at ease—to reduce his or her anxieties.

BUILDING CREDIBILITY

Work at developing and maintaining credibility with your students, their teachers and their parents. If your students and others doubt your ideas and competencies, your chances of success will be minimal.

Developing credibility depends upon many things. If you can deliver on your promises, you will go a long way toward attaining it. For this reason you must take care to avoid promising too much.

Encourage your students to believe that success is possible. However, if you promise greater improvement than can be achieved within a given time, in addition to damaging your credibility you may create a serious obstacle to the student's motivation. It is best to avoid promising in advance that particular reading skills will be acquired in a given time.

Your students' achievements in reading will pretty much speak for themselves. Of course, students, parents and teachers will appreciate your comments on each success, and sincerely deserved praise will serve as motivation for further efforts.

Trust

The main ingredient in the development of credibility is *trust*. Communications specialists* suggest that trust is maximized when your students:

---

*David Johnson, *Reaching Out*, Englewood Cliffs, New Jersey, Prentice Hall, 1974, p. 45. This is an excellent book with exercises for learning about the dynamics of developing trusting relationships with others.

1. are aware that *if* they are open with you and try to follow your directions, this could possibly lead to beneficial results for them;

2. realize that both you and they contribute to either success or failure of your joint projects;

3. believe that they have more to gain by working with you than by not working with you; and

4. feel relatively confident that you will behave in such a way that no harm will result to them.

Providing Feedback

In order to create feelings of trust and to avoid student defensiveness, you should consider the following guidelines for providing feedback to students:*

1. *Focus most of your comments on their behaviors and their observable accomplishments and problems.* For example, you might say, "John, you read nearly forty words correctly in this paragraph and made only four mistakes."

---

*The main ideas here have been adapted by permission of the publishers from David Johnson, Ibid., pp. 16-17.

2.   *Avoid providing inferential interpretations and judgements of what such mistakes mean to you.* Don't give a diagnosis to a student such as, "You are a dyslectic," or "You are learning disabled." Labels often confuse and do great disservice to effective communication.

3.   *Focus most of your feedback on description.* To *describe* what the student has done in your presence is to be neutral. On the other hand, *judgement* is evaluative and personal. Since judgement is evaluation in terms of good or bad, right or wrong, and is personally taken, provide few judgements and when you do, balance negative criticism with positive remarks.

4.   *Focus your comments on specific situations—the more recent, the better.* Your comments will be received most meaningfully if you give them as soon as it is appropriate to do so. Do not save up your comments.

5.   *Your comments should be given in such a way that they are viewed as your sharing of ideas rather than giving advice.* When ideas are shared the student feels less threatened. It is unfortunate how often people fail to realize that their advice is received as a kind of "put-down."

6.   *The sharing of ideas is more easily developed when alternatives are explored rather than solutions or*

answers given. When suggesting books to be read or exercises for reading, give the student opportunities to make his or her own choices wherever possible, by providing a variety of choice.

7. *Present information or comments that you believe the student can use—rather than the amount of information you might like to give to the student.* Do not overload the student with your ideas about reading and schools. The feedback should be based on its input-value to the receiver—not on its release-value to you.

STUDENT PROBLEMS

Since your student is likely to be especially anxious during your first meeting, your first contact is *not* the time to discuss the student's reading problems—or even to be too aggressive in trying to build a friendly relationship. These things will follow in time, after you have proved to the student that your goal is to help and that you are on his or her "side." Allow all discussions of problems to develop in the natural course of testing and tutoring sessions. Should the student start out by volunteering information about his or her reading difficulties, simply state, "We can work together on that and I'm here to help in any way I can."

Be Pleasant But Businesslike

Be pleasant but businesslike. On your first meeting with the student, say something like, "As you know, we're going to be working together on your reading. In order to help you, I need to find out exactly how you read; so when you read for me today, *don't worry* about making mistakes—just read the best you can." Assure the student that any scores derived will not be "grades," but *measurements* that can be compared to later measurement, which will show his or her improvement. Indicate that you will use the first results to decide on what methods and materials will be of the most help in your tutoring sessions.

Student Questions

While you should not ignore questions or comments from the student at the first session, it is best to give only brief, casual responses. Move directly into the testing process as described in Part C. This approach eliminates awkwardness that can be associated with superficial conversation—the only kind of exchange possible unless you already know the student—but it also helps to by-pass (or at least minimize) preliminary struggles of will between the two of you. Any negativity or unwillingness to cooperate on the student's part will thus be met by your obvious optimism. By taking it for granted that he or she will perform as expected, you can usually avoid a confrontation.

YOUR FIRST DIAGNOSIS

Because diagnostic checks necessarily start at a reading level far below the student's age-grade level, he or she will find the first exercise easier than expected. When a student has finished, express your thanks and add some kind of specific comment on something you can honestly praise—such as, "You're very good at noticing periods." A word of encouragement can do wonders to dispel tension; also the fact that you make no verbal corrections while he or she is reading will tend to help the student feel more secure.

Depending on the pupil's age and attention span, you can either proceed through all the assessment tests at the first sitting or complete them in two sessions. With younger students and with those who are more distractible, you may find it advisable to start every single session with some kind of measurement or check-up before moving to the day's reading exercises, as a means of focusing attention on immediate tasks.

SUMMARY

In summary, your first contact with a new student should be geared to setting you both at ease in a direct, professional relationship that will aid you in taking charge without using overly authoritarian methods.

While tempered with cordial comments and any kind of praise you can give *sincerely*, your approach to the student should show that you expect cooperation and that your main goal is to help. Your attitude should communicate friendliness and respect for the student as an individual, and the fact that you seriously desire to be of service. In most cases, students will respond to your sincerity by giving their best attention and effort to the project that the two of you will be sharing.

5

Individual Differences

Before attempting to help a student who has reading problems, most educators require some measurement of the student's general and specific abilities to learn. The most commonly-used measurement is the I.Q. score yielded by an intelligence test. Not all psychologists, however, hold the same views on what intelligence is, how it should be measured, and how I.Q. scores should be used.

LEARNING APTITUDES

There is an unfortunate amount of disagreement today, among lay people and professionals alike, over what "intelligence" tests measure. However, since they are often a part of school measurement, we should recognize that the crucial issue is how intelligence tests should be used. I.Q. scores can be used in ways known to be actually harmful to children. If used properly, they can be of considerable value to diagnostic and prescriptive work. Administered and thoroughly interpreted by trained persons, intelligence tests can be useful indicators of the general level of a student's current functioning on various academic tasks.

Commonly used intelligence tests include measurements of a student's language and mathematical skills. Among the skills tested, language tasks are usually the most important because they are the most predictive of general school performance.

Nevertheless, we believe it to be a myth that general or specialized tests of intelligence, aptitude, or achievement can measure one's intellectual competence in all situations. A person's problem-solving skills shift from task to task. We also believe that on any given task, an individual's performance can vary widely. People can become "smarter" or less able in the sense that they can become more or less proficient in solving problems.

It is your duty as a tutor to help students acquire those intellectual tools which can genuinely help them become more efficient at solving their problems. Reading skills are helpful, if not crucial, to being reasonably intelligent in this world. By helping a student to read better, you are making it possible for him or her to behave more intelligently now and in the future.

When your student has learned to read at a proficient level, you can have considerable confidence that he or she will be able to learn easily. A poor showing on an intelligence test is no reason for placing a permanent score on any student's "intelligence;" *intelligence is not a permanent, unchangeable characteristic.*

It is the school's task–and yours–to help students behave more intelligently. As important as heredity is, environment greatly influences how well or poorly any person performs. You can help or hinder the abilities of students to solve their school problems; as a tutor you will be an important part of their environment.

Our directions for helping a student gain increased ability are simple.

1. In order to concentrate on appropriate problem areas, utilize experts for diagnosing reading problems whenever possible.

2. Avoid negative attitudes and punishments which can make a student insecure and so handicap his or her development.

3. With the help of professional diagnosis and advice, practice methods of teaching reading that have demonstrated success in the past.

THE READING SPECIALIST

The professional reading diagnostician usually has at least a master's degree in reading and often has had a year or more of advanced work leading to a doctor's degree. Unfortunately, not all schools have reading clinics with staffs of professional reading diagnosticians. In nearly all cases where specialized reading clinics are available in a school, students with reading problems will have—and should have—been referred to it by their teachers. If the school has requested your services as a tutor, there is a great likelihood that diagnostic results have already been obtained. However, should a student fail to make expected progress after a semester of tutoring, further clinical assessment should be recommended.

The professional examiner will more than likely have administered a diagnostic test such as the *Durrell Analysis of Reading Difficulty.* In order to administer this test, one must be specially trained. It is a long test, but it is comprehensive in furnishing specific, needed information about an individual's reading abilities. The test measures: 1) oral reading, which includes speed, types of errors, and comprehension; 2) silent reading, which includes speed and recall; 3) listening comprehension (graded paragraphs are read to the student and then they are asked specific questions); 4) word recognition and word analysis; 5) naming letters, identifying letters named, and matching letters; 6) visual memory of words (primary); 7) sounds (hearing sounds in words and sounds in letters); 8) learning to hear sounds in words; 9) sounds of letters; 10) visual memory of words (intermediate); 11) phonic spelling of words; and 12) spelling ability.

The examiner may also administer group or other individual diagnostic tests to determine how the scores on one instrument might compare with scores on the other.

A good examiner will seldom rely on one test for a diagnosis. Sound diagnostic practice requires the use of more than one test instrument.

The examiner will also have a series of reading textbooks so that an "informal reading test" can be administered. On this test, the examiner merely opens a textbook to a page at random and asks the student to read. Two or three books may be used, each written at different grade levels, to determine at what level the student can read quickly, accurately, and comfortably.

LEARNING DISABILITIES

There are few phrases in education which are more misunderstood than the phrase "learning disabilities." Many different definitions of learning disability have been offered by educators, thus contributing to the confusion. However, all of the definitions recognize one basic condition: there are students "with a problem in understanding or in using spoken or written language."* As further stated in a publication of the Association for Children with

---

Specific Learning Disabilities . . . A First Look for Parents, published by Kiwanis International in cooperation with Association for Children with Learning Disabilities, 1975.

Learning Disabilities: "Some disabilities are referred to as 'specific' learning disabilities . . . to differentiate them from other disabilities, which are primarily due to mental retardation, emotional disturbance, poor vision or poor hearing, or cultural disadvantage. The child with a specific learning disability is of average or above intellect."*

Among the more commonly discussed types of "specific learning disability" is *dyslexia*, which some assume to be a type of minimal brain disfunction. Others prefer the terms, "perceptual handicap" or "neurological handicap." In any event, as a tutor you will face these terms and perhaps the conditions to which they refer.

Dyslexia

Dyslexia has been defined as "inability to learn to read, or word blindness." It must be stressed here that this is a very difficult condition for even the most competent experts to diagnose. In fact, authorities themselves have not yet agreed upon what actually constitutes dyslexia. What they do agree upon is that, despite years of reading instruction in school, some children do not learn to read adequately. When such children do learn to read even at a very low level, their reading is a slow and painful process. Some specialists feel that such reading difficulties are

*Ibid.

caused by a malfunctioning of the brain. Brain malfunction is usually discovered through an EEG (electroencephalogram), which is a record of brain wave patterns. It must be emphasized that the brain wave patterns of most students with reading problems are within the normal range.

One of the reasons we hesitate to use the label "dyslexia" in reference to any student is that the diagnosis tends to suggest a possible congenital condition which is beyond correction. Unfortunately, in some cases educators and parents alike have been misled by the label into believing a dyslexic student cannot be helped.

Whatever the diagnosis, trying to help a student learn to read better will almost always bring about some measure of improvement.

After he or she has been carefully tested for visual, hearing, glandular and neurological defects, a student may be diagnosed dyslectic. Here are some characteristics commonly associated with the term dyslexia. The student:

1. may be frequently confused about time, distance, direction, and size;

2. may have difficulty discriminating between sounds and may not seem to hear certain sounds—which can cause difficulty in learning to reproduce sounds correctly;

3. may have trouble telling right from left; and

4. may seem unable to remember words even after
    they have been taught repeatedly (and even after
    being instructed as to their sounds, forms, and
    meanings). Prompted on a word in one line, the
    child may not remember the same word in the
    next line.

The best technique to use with a dyslectic person (as
with any person with a reading disability) is to begin at a
very low level, where he or she can continually experience
success even though moving at a snail's pace. The instruc-
tor must make sure that the student has thoroughly mastered the skills at one level before proceeding to another
level.

For example, if you want a student to learn the consonant sound "b," stick with the sound until it is recognized every single time it is seen. This will mean much review of material taught, but it will be worth the effort.

Always bear in mind that you will have to be satisfied with small successes in the beginning. If you try to
teach too much at one time, you will only confuse and
frustrate the student to the point that all will be lost.

Going through the assessment procedures suggested in
this book may help you to understand what the exact
reading problem is. If a student happens to fit many of the
categories of dyslexia, don't despair; you will simply have

to work a little harder, go at a slower pace, and repeat frequently what you are absolutely sure was mastered.

If you find that a student is unable to tell time or to determine distance, direction, and size, it will be wise to bring these concepts into focus, not necessarily just at reading time, but as frequently as possible. If you are fully aware that the condition exists, you will understand that your student is not to be blamed for failure to learn.

Some students learn reading concepts quite readily and almost incidentally, but others do not. Consider for example the following case:

Case Study of Patty . . .

Patty is an alert sixth grade student. During her first year of school, she had been successful at learning to read. Her second grade experience was quite unfortunate. She did not gain a year in reading. Patty had become fearful of failure; she refused to attempt to read. Consequently, when she entered third grade, still reading at a first grade level, she was sent to the remedial reading teacher. That specialist described her as "highly distractible and lacking in interest in learning to read." The teacher noted Patty had quickly learned the technique of avoidance by having other students do the assigned classroom work for her.

When she was in fourth grade, her mother, Mrs. S__, enrolled Patty in a private reading clinic. There she was diagnosed as having dyslexia, and for an entire year she left school during part of each day to attend this clinic. During the other part of the day, she was seen by the school remedial reading teacher and received help from her regular classroom teacher.

At the end of the school year, Patty was dismissed from the clinic because the teachers felt they could not help her; she was now reading at a second grade level.

Mrs. S___ had informed the clinic that Patty's father had a severe reading problem, and that even as an adult, he was a virtual nonreader. She said her husband was employed in a job that required little reading and that she helped him when necessary. As a result, the clinic personnel diagnosed Patty's reading problem as partly family related and suggested to Mrs. S___ that she help Patty accept her reading problem and not "feel badly" about it.

As a result, Patty began freely to tell people she "couldn't read" and completely avoided trying. Patty's teachers did not agree that she was unable to learn reading, and they expected the same assignments from her as they did from the other students. However, all of Patty's "good" friends continued to do her work for her, and her achievement level dropped even lower than it was when she was in fourth grade.

Did this defeatist attitude help Patty? Who can say for sure that the girl's reading problem is *en famille*? We are unwilling to accept such a claim; but even if it were true, we could not justify either shrugging it off or stressing it as an "unchangeable" condition.

When we began working on this case, we aggressively encouraged both the student and her mother to gain confidence in Patty's individual abilities. Then, using a systematic, step-by-step process, we sorted out which skills the student already possessed for reading and which ones she lacked. This enabled us to work up a program for Patty's mother to follow with her. As a result, Patty began to show real progress, which stimulated her to greater effort and also reassured her mother. At present, there is every indication that Patty will gradually raise her reading ability to a satisfactory level.

Lateral Dominance

Lateral dominance, the side of the body which dominates, has been considered by some educators to be a factor in reading disability.

Is the student left handed or right handed? Is the left eye dominant over the right eye? It has been noted that some students who have not established dominance (who use right and left hands interchangeably) and some who have crossed dominance (right eyed, left handed), also have difficulty learning to read. However, there is considerable disagreement as to whether or not lack of dominance can be considered as a cause of reading problems.

There was a time when students who preferred to use the left hand were forced to use the right hand—a practice which frequently produced mixed dominance, with children growing up using both hands. In the past, some authorities suggested that training left handed persons to be right handed was a cause of reading problems. As a consequence, many people still believe that mixed lateral dominance causes reading failure despite the fact that most professionals no longer believe this to be true. However, since there is disagreement and the data is inconclusive, we would certainly suggest that you be open-minded about what future research will conclude.

Whatever the case, it has been shown that large numbers of students with mixed lateral dominance can learn to read with no difficulty. Furthermore, any students who lack lateral dominance can be helped to read better. We have found it to be no great barrier in teaching reading skills to formerly poor readers.

MOTIVATION

The reading specialist will also attempt to make an assessment of each student's desire (or lack of desire) to perform well. Most poor readers have low motivation because of poor estimates of their reading abilities, i.e., they have feelings of incompetence. And feelings of incompetence in reading results from the reactions of others to their failures. For most poor readers, a major handicap they must overcome is a lack of confidence in their abilities which almost invariably have been the result of having been criticized and stigmatized for failure. You will need to continually encourage self-assurance.

TEACHING EFFECTIVENESS

We hesitate to include ineffective teaching as a possible cause of reading failure because it is often used as an easy excuse without a basis in fact. However, we must admit we have seen a few classrooms in which necessary reading skills are not taught effectively.

At the other extreme, there are those classrooms in which nearly every child, regardless of social class, race, sex, or physical characteristics, learns to read at a level in advance of his or her age. Fortunately, the majority of teachers do a very good job with most students. However, most teachers are burdened with large numbers of students, and that is where your supplementary tutoring services can be of great value.

Occasionally we have seen teachers who were relatively successful at teaching reading skills, but who did not encourage student interests in reading. It is important to realize that both reading skill and interest in reading are learned characteristics. As a tutor, you will have the opportunity to enhance interest in reading through individualized work.

It is important to consider the teacher's point of view. The great majority of teachers are conscientious and dedicated to helping each student as much as possible. Most teachers also believe they are well experienced and trained, and criticisms from tutors, unless requested, may be considered as interference. You may wish to concentrate on supplementing the teacher's efforts without criticizing his or her teaching methods.

Also, keep in mind that teachers are often under a great deal of pressure. They are constantly being evaluated in terms of how well they cover a rather broad curriculum. Teachers who are responsible for mathematics, reading, science, spelling, English, social studies, art, music, library time, recess, physical education (and any other special subject that may come along) find that their days are filled to capacity. Thus, it should be understandable when a teacher has relatively little time to devote to an individual student who has fallen behind in reading.

Tutoring is your chance to be of real help. In any case, there is much more to be gained from eliciting cooperation than from incurring resentment.

PART B

PRIVATE TUTORING SERVICES

6

Private Practice

In communities where tutoring is not furnished through the schools, tutors must seek clientele by offering their services directly to parents. Sometimes several tutors combine their services in a tutoring center, where such problems as location, appointment scheduling, fee-setting, advertising and collection are handled by a central office in exchange for some percentage of each tutor's earnings at the center. Should you become affiliated with a tutoring service, you will be expected to conform to the center's rules regarding procedures with schools, students and parents.

If you are establishing an independent practice, however, it will be necessary to set up your own system of procedures. Following are some suggestions for organizing and setting up an independent practice.

PRELIMINARY CONSIDERATIONS

Before you begin offering services on a private basis, make sure you fulfill the main requirements for success in tutoring.

Where school-furnished tutorial and other services are available, most parents who seek private tutoring prefer to pay for the service rather than have their children placed in special classes, or singled out for tutoring within the school situation. Also, in circumstances where teachers have too many students and special tutoring services are not available, parents will seek outside assistance. In either case, there are parents who will view private tutoring as having some special value for their children and while they expect to pay for it, they also demand assurance that positive results can be achieved.

Consequently, if you want to become a private tutor, you should be well prepared by training and experience to provide successful tutoring. Tutoring is a serious business in terms of its consequences for children. Inadequacy on your part might add to a student's difficulties. Hence, we suggest that if you have had no tutoring experience, you begin by offering your services at a school or tutoring service where professional directions and supervision are available, either at minimum rates or as a volunteer, in order to build up experience and establish a reputation for success.

REFERENCES

Sound experience will serve as a basis for providing references. You should be able to provide at least three recent references from parents of students you have tutored--or, if your experience has been with a school system (whether paid or voluntary), from satisfied teachers and supervisors. Do not provide names of references (either on your fact sheet or in verbal interviews) without first obtaining permission from those whose names you are using.

SEEKING REFERRALS

Among your most important sources of students in need of tutoring are principals and teachers and sometimes librarians. These individuals are frequently asked by parents to give advice about reading problems; they are also invaluable sources of information you may need in your work.

When going on record as a private tutor at either a school or a library, offer a written (preferably typed) sheet or file card containing the following: 1) grade levels you tutor; 2) your credentials; 3) pertinent information about yourself; 4) references; 5) hours available for tutoring; 6) place of tutoring; and 7) telephone numbers through which you can be reached at specific times. Like your advertisement, this information should be concise and factual—neither a lengthy resume nor a "sales pitch."

To establish cordial relationships at a school, first telephone the principal's office with a request that you be allowed to present yourself as an independent reading tutor who wants to cooperate with the school in every possible way. Almost any principal will find time to interview you personally and many principals will introduce you to other faculty members.

When talking to school personnel, always make it clear that *they* are the authorities and that your aim is merely to offer professional services not available in the classroom. This point, in addition to being a statement of fact, is important in dispelling potential resentment on the part of some educators who might otherwise tend to regard you as an intruder.

By offering your full cooperation, and by asking to be allowed to consult the principal or a teacher for background information and suggestions concerning students from their school, you will establish your own professional status. A student whose parents have hired you because of a school recommendation is likely to receive in-school encouragement not enjoyed by a student who is being tutored by a stranger to the school personnel.

ADVERTISING

The important point here is to be professional. Once your practice has been established, if you are successful your reputation as a tutor will spread by word-of-mouth. Where you feel advertising is necessary it should be in the form of an announcement of services as in the case with doctors and lawyers.

Any announcements you make should always mention your relevant experiences and credentials. If you are a student, give your major subjects and offer references from teachers; if you are a former teacher, name grades you have taught and degrees earned; your willingness to provide references should be noted; and be sure to include your tutoring experience.

Your announcements, to repeat, must present a professional image. Do not exaggerate or make claims that you can "cure" reading problems. Do not make a "sales pitch." Simply list the types of services you offer and your relevant experience and credentials.

LOCATION

A student's home is usually the worst possible location for tutoring. By all means, if you cannot use school facilities (and if you tutor independently, you generally cannot), utilize an isolated spot in your own home or manage to rent a small amount of space for a percentage of what you earn as a tutor. The area required is minimal; it need be only large enough to hold a table, two chairs and a wastebasket; but you *must* be able to work in it without interruption.

Freedom from interruption is the main reason for tutoring outside the student's home, but also it is advisable to use surroundings that are unfamiliar to the student. This is one advantage independent tutoring has over school-sponsored tutoring, since the school environment can serve for some students as an unhappy reminder of past failures.

In any case, you should provide a setting and an atmosphere that are "special" and private; it is best to make yourself unavailable to all outside interference, including telephone calls.

FEES AND APPOINTMENTS

Lacking the advantages of a fee schedule and collection services as provided by a tutoring center, you should set definite rules concerning payment for private tutoring and stick to them closely.

If you do not know the "going" hourly rate for tutoring in your community, ask the educators you are contacting for help in getting started. Whatever fee schedule you decide on, *charge it with consistency*. In those cases where the client is unable to afford more than two sessions a week when three sessions are needed, it is usually wiser to give the student extra time during the two sessions his parents can afford than to make an exception by lowering your fee.

Your fee schedule can include a reduced rate for group tutoring (maximum of three students in a group). In such cases the private fee is not to be divided by the number of students in the group, but reduced by twenty to twenty-five percent for each student. Thus, small group tutoring brings more compensation, commensurate to the additional work it involves. Of course, if you believe that a certain student requires one-to-one tutoring, you should not recommend small group tutoring sessions. On the other hand, certain students might benefit more from small group sessions.

When beginning your practice, it is advisable to collect payment by-the-session. You can explain to parents that you have no facilities for setting up a bookkeeping and billing system, and that cash payment will eliminate use of debits and credits when appointments have to be changed or cancelled. You will find the majority of parents cooperative in this regard

Some tutoring centers contract with parents for a set number of tutoring hours, and insist on payment of the full contract whether or not the student attends regularly. Usually, under this agreement it is possible for appointments to be rescheduled, provided the parent telephones the day before there is to be an absence.

As an independent tutor, you should agree to take a student for a specific (minimum) period of time considered necessary for accomplishing measurable reading improvement; and you should ask that arrangements be made in advance to reschedule any cancelled appointments. If appointments are skipped entirely, unless notified in advance you should charge for the time that was scheduled for the student; however, should an appointment be cancelled in time for you to schedule another student, no charge should be made. This arrangement, used by physicians and dentists, is fair to both you and the client, since under it you, too, are free to cancel or change an appointment should you encounter a personal emergency. When illness or another unavoidable circumstance will prevent your keeping an appointment, be sure to extend the same courtesy you expect, by notifying the client in plenty of time for the student's plans to be changed.

DIAGNOSIS

Unless you are qualified to do diagnostic work, it is advisable that you make sure each student is examined by professionals before you begin tutoring. In most cases (given the necessary permission from parents), teachers and principals are willing to give a tutor general test results on vision, hearing, aptitudes and achievement. Also, you can ask for the results of any recent reading evaluation the school may have made. Additionally, it is your business to know whether or not the student has any type of physical disability that might affect reading skills. When these kinds of information have not been gathered (if you are not a professionally trained reading specialist), you should ask the parents to have the student tested at a reading clinic prior to acceptance for tutoring.

The professional diagnosis will enable you to start tutoring with an appropriate assessment of the student's reading skills and with his or her individual reading problems already pinpointed—thus making it possible for you to begin tutoring for immediate results. In addition, such a diagnosis can protect you from making mistakes, because it can furnish important facts which might be discernible only through a professional evaluation procedure.

However, even though you have a professional diagnosis made available to you, you should still carry out the assessment of reading skills exercises suggested in Part C of this book. By such assessments, you will gain an insight into the professional diagnosis and be provided with an important means for developing rapport with students. Your assessments will also allow you to measure the growth that your students make under your guidance.

7

Community Resources

A student with reading problems should be examined by specialists or experts whose training has enabled them to pinpoint causes for an individual's lack of achievement. Routine physical and educational screening examinations given in school are helpful but are not always thorough enough. It is true that such examinations often alert us to the presence of handicaps; but some youngsters have physical, emotional, social, and instructional impairments which are subtle and difficult to discern.

Expert examination may be crucial to proper treatment. Successful treatment of reading failure frequently depends upon identifying conditions—sometimes complex ones—that are currently impeding learning. Determining the main reasons for a student's difficulty can, in many cases, help you plan his or her tutoring program. If a parent has retained you for tutoring services, be sure to inquire if vision, hearing and health examinations have been made recently by specialists. You should also inquire about social and emotional conditions which may be related to the student's reading problems.

The rest of this chapter discusses several important areas which warrant the obtaining of professional services prior to tutoring.

VISION SERVICES

*Determine whether or not the student's vision has
been checked by an ophthalmologist or optometrist.* It
may be that he or she is not seeing letters and words clearly. Types of visual problems which may interfere with
reading are: *hyperopia* (farsightedness), *myopia* (nearsightedness), and *astigmatism* (blurring of vision due to a defect
in the eye).

Hyperopia

The student with hyperopia sees better at a distance
than at close range. Farsighted persons typically seek to
avoid close reading as well as written work at their seats.
The teacher may not be aware of this visual problem (since
such students can read from the chalkboard) and may sus-
pect the pupil of avoiding assignments. To compound this
situation, such pupils may, by straining their eyes, see
close work reasonably well for a short time. Parents have
additional difficulty noticing farsightedness because their
children can watch television without any apparent difficulty. This subtle visual problem can be detected and corrected by an ophthalmologist or optometrist. The greatest
problem may be to get a farsighted youngster to wear his
or her glasses for close work.

Myopia

On the other hand, the myopic student is easily identified through the visual screening at school. This person has difficulty seeing at a distance. The nearsighted student usually squints in order to see the chalkboard and sits quite close to the television set at home. Lens correction is so helpful to nearsightedness that most students with this type of eye problem will wear their glasses without too much prodding.

Astigmatism

Astigmatism is not readily identified through the normal vision screening at school. If a student complains of blurred vision, an eye specialist should be consulted. This type of visual problem may cause inability to distinguish between similar letters or numbers, such as *b* and *d*, *p* and *g, m* and *n*, or *3* and *8*. Astigmatism can also be corrected by glasses.

There are other types of visual problems. Muscle imbalance (crossed or nonfocusing eyes), cateracts, and glaucoma are possible in students, but the three conditons first described are the most common visual difficulties. Any visual problem should be diagnosed and corrected as quickly as possible. To wait too long will only cause discomfort, confusion, and a definite loss of valuable instruction time at school and at home.

HEARING SERVICES

Determine whether or not the student's hearing has been checked by an audiologist. In many cities, if the schools do not supply this service, there are speech and hearing clinics that provide this service at little or no cost. One may have difficulty in detecting a hearing problem because a student has learned to compensate for a hearing loss by pretending, lip-reading, or some other method. A person must be able to hear sounds accurately in order to learn to read well. Some characteristics of the student with a hearing loss are:

1. Facial contortions or blank expressions;

2. Responding inappropriately to spoken directions when unable to see the face of the speaker;

3. Complaints of inattentiveness from the student's teacher or others;

4. Repeated responses of "ma'am," "sir," "huh?," "what," and similar indications of not hearing requests;

5. Obvious clues such as turning an ear toward the speaker, or putting a hand behind an ear in order to gain a better understanding of what is being said;

6. Generally poor school achievement because of inability to understand many of the directions; and

7. Difficulty in recognizing differences between sounds, especially such sounds as those made by the letters *b*, *t* and *d* or *m* and *n*.

An audiologist can almost always detect the difficulties and recommend what should be done.

Should an audiologist fail to find any physical impairment, you must still be alert to possible hearing problems. Watch for ear infections and colds. Some students have trouble hearing only during an illness. There are some who have passed hearing tests, then have become ill with ear infections that cause hearing loss. During this period, the student is not able to pay proper attention to directions at school and is easily distracted.

There are many students whose ears must be drained on a regular basis. If a student's ear passages tend to become clogged frequently, watch for periods when he or she does not respond normally to sound or voices; it may be time for a trip to the doctor's office. If you are tutoring in a school situation, the student's teacher should be made aware of this condition so that it can be verified and parental action can be recommended. Teachers sometimes identify symptoms of illness not recognized by parents. This happened in the following case of Kim, a first grader:

Kim was shy and withdrawn with her teacher and the other children in the classroom. She was not learning to read even though she had high achievement scores on her kindergarten tests. In the teachers' lounge one day, the first grade teacher was puzzling about Kim, and the child's former kindergarten teacher overheard her comments. "You cannot possibly be talking about Kim B__, the happy and outgoing child I knew last year," she said.

As a result of this conversation with the previous teacher, Kim's first grade teacher decided to ask the child's mother to come to school.

Kim's mother said she suspected a hearing problem, but had "not gotten around to" taking her to a doctor since Kim had not made any serious complaints at home. Fortunately, the next day her problem was quickly diagnosed by an ear specialist as a recurrence of a middle ear infection, and the little girl was quickly helped back to good health and good performance in school.

A teacher asked us to observe a student in her room. She stated that on some days the student literally screamed at her and the other pupils, and learned very little. On other days, when the student was quiet, she seemed to learn rapidly.

One of the things we did was to stand behind the student and talk to her in a normal tone. She made no response at all. We immediately suspected that she was not hearing correctly and called a speech and hearing center for an emergency appointment with an audiologist. The results of the examination revealed that the girl had a severe hearing loss in her right ear and that the hearing in her left ear was not completely normal.

We suspected that this girl, like Kim, might have a middle ear infection which would cause her hearing to be better on some days than on others. An ear specialist was called. The doctor cleared up the infection, and later the audiologist fitted the youngster's right ear with a hearing aid. These corrective measures had dramatic results in the form of a happier and more alert student who rapidly, with tutorial assistance, became capable of normal classroom performance.

Students with hearing problems usually need special help in listening. You can teach most hard-of-hearing students to be good listeners. If a student is deaf or hard of hearing, it is especially important that you and others regularly carry on long conversations with him or her. These conversations should focus on events and people of interest to the student.

Avoid emphasizing (or perhaps even discussing) reading or hearing problems. Pay full attention to the student's interests without acting like a judge. Showing sincere interest, subtly try to get him or her to tell you what happened during the day; discuss what the student liked or disliked about school that day. Read stories and talk about them; ask for and openly show respect for your student's opinions—even when they differ from your own.

Remember, when you talk to the hard-of-hearing, young or old, make sure that you have the person's attention. Try to make good eye contact and talk normally. An audiologist or a speech pathologist can give excellent and specific advice for improving communication with a hard-of-hearing person.

HEALTH SERVICES

Determine whether or not the student has had a thorough physical examination by a physician. Some students are tired and listless most of the day in school. They do not have sufficient energy to get through a school day successfully, thus little work is accomplished. A physician may check for thyroid abnormalities. A student with hyperthyroidism will be overactive and irritable, and will tire easily; the student with hypothyroidism will be underactive and will tend to be overweight and sluggish. Other kinds of thyroid imbalance can cause learning problems.

Allergies cause other physical conditions that can drain a person's energy but they may not be easily recognized except by an allergist. Many parents and teachers are unaware of their children's allergies, mistaking allergic reactions for colds or flu.

An example of the allergic child was furnished by Tim, a sixth grade student who had little interest in school. He did not participate in sports or other school related activities and he was quite overweight for his age. He was often absent from school because of what appeared to be a series of colds. When in school, he frequently had his head on his desk. His eyes sometimes watered and he occasionally had a rash around his mouth. The school psychologist and reading specialist found Tim to be extremely intelligent, but at a reading level approximately two years below his actual grade placement. Both experts also reported that it was difficult for Tim to complete their tests because of apparent fatigue and sluggishness.

Tim's mother expressed sincere concern, but was at a loss as to what to do. She had taken Tim to their family doctor, a general practitioner, who reported him to be in normal health. Since we had seen similar cases, one of our first questions to Tim's mother was, "Have you ever taken him to an allergist?" She replied, "I'll try anything," and immediately called her family doctor for a recommendation to a specialist in allergies.

The allergist, on examining the boy, found him to be highly allergic to milk, soda pop, flour, tomatoes, and other things he had been eating for many years. When Tim was given a diet free of these foods, his cold symptoms decreased; in addition, a remarkable improvement in learning occurred. Not only did the boy's face clear up and his sluggishness disappear; he began to take an active interest in school. His reading quickly improved as he began to read more. Consequently, his parents and teachers were more capable of giving him the added help he needed.

For most individuals, learning to read is a task demanding considerable energy; therefore, it is essential for them to be physically well, alert, and attentive.

SCHOOL SERVICES

Determine whether or not the student has been seen recently by a school psychologist, counselor or school social worker. If services of school psychologists, counselors or social workers are available in your school district, the type of services offered will depend on their training and experience. In some school districts, counselors, school psychologists and social workers have had extensive training in reading diagnosis and prescriptive instruction.

Actually, results depend on the skills available among all staff members. Some school psychologists are expected merely to administer intelligence tests; others are expected to provide only consultation services to teachers. In some localities, school systems hire psychometrists who administer psychological tests, plus school psychologists who receive these test results and interpret them to parents and teachers. There are also school psychologists who are more concerned about the emotional health of students than about their reading achievement.

However, most school psychologists are equipped to administer and interpret a variety of tests measuring intelligence, reading, spelling, and arithmetic achievement, perceptual skills, and vocational interests. In addition they are often trained to provide an assessment of the social and emotional conditions associated with learning failure.

Following is a typical example of how one school psychologist partially described a student's social and emotional situation in school:

"Bobby's teacher decided after one month of school that she needed help with him. He came to school the first day upset and crying because of a fight on the bus. Mrs. T__, his new second grade teacher, talked to Bobby and calmed him down for a while, but he spent an unhappy day at school. His early morning altercation continued during recess and at lunch. The second day of school was better, but he was easily upset when the boy next to him accidentally bumped him. When assignments were given to the class and the teacher was ready for her reading group, Bobby shouted that he didn't know what to do. Mrs. T__ found that Bobby couldn't read the second grade book, and that he stumbled with the words in a first grade book.

Bobby's days in second grade varied from extreme emotional upset to somewhat calm days. He was not successfully motivated to read or to do his written assignments. If he discovered that academic work was difficult for him, he would become agitated and push it aside. He would also poke children next to him, scribble on their papers, and trip anyone who came near him. The other children began to dislike and avoid Bobby. This tended to make him even more hostile and irritable during the day.

"After Mrs. T___described Bobby, I [the psychologist] asked if I could observe him in the schoolroom. On the day I visited, Bobby came into the room by banging the door and announcing loudly that he had arrived. This caused all the other children to groan loudly, and Bobby reacted by hitting the girl closest to him and making her cry. Mrs. T__, after gaining control of the situation, proceeded to start the day."

Emotional problems frequently interfere with a students ability to learn to read. Just as frequently, reading handicaps can result in various emotional problems. It is often extremely difficult to discern which problem is the cause and which is the result. When reading problems and emotional problems exist together, however, it is necessary that you become aware of both and attempt to deal with each in an appropriate way—given your own skills and limitations.

Students may react to reading disabilities by simply avoiding any activities that involve reading. The more parents and teachers demand work from such student's the more they tend to withdraw. We have seen high school boys and girls who read at a second grade level spending entire school days sitting in the back of the classroom, doing absolutely nothing. They will often prop a book up in front of them and hide behind it, hoping the teacher will not ask them any questions or expect any written work from them. Frequently, the teacher will be forced to go along with such behavior knowing that these pupils, with their current skills, cannot do the work and are beyond their help in the classroom (given the number of students present and available resources). If they are quiet and do not bother the teacher or other students, they may even receive a passing grade, resulting in their moving on to the next subject or the next grade—where the same process of failure may be repeated.

Other students may react aggressively to their own lack of reading skills. At home, when a parent tries to persuade them to do their school work, they become hostile and angry and react to the whole family in such an unpleasant manner that it soon becomes easier to ignore the whole situation. In school, such students may become class bullies. They may laugh at other students and taunt them as they read or work at other school-related tasks. No matter how hard the teacher tries to help, they may reject both the work and the teacher.

There are many other ways students develop negative emotional responses to school work. A student may experience repeated failures at the beginning reading level, or suffer ridicule from other students because of reading errors; also lack of confidence in other areas can affect reading performance. Whatever may trigger them, negative emotional responses can limit a student's ability to learn.

Teachers, school psychologists and/or school social workers, if properly trained, can provide advice to parents and to you on strategies that can reduce social and emotional causes of learning problems. As a private tutor, do not hesitate to have a student's parents seek such services if they are available through the school. Professional persons often have so many requests and demands for their services that a student's problem is sometimes deferred. But if you and your student's parents are cooperative, patient and helpful, professional school people will usually be more than willing to provide you with their assistance.

It is in your student's interest, and it is ethically imperative, that you help parents have good relationships with their children's teachers and other school people.

PART C

THE ASSESSMENT OF READING PROBLEMS

8

Measuring Comprehension

In assessing the comprehension skills of students you will need to be concerned with the levels at which they can read.

ASSESSING READING LEVELS

As you begin working with a student, you will discover the benefits of knowing three distinct reading levels: they are the *frustration, instruction* and *independent levels.*

The three levels are defined by the following example.

Mary, a student in the fourth grade, is confused and frustrated when trying to read fourth grade level materials, even though she is able to read and understand many single words at that level. The fourth grade level is Mary's *frustration level* of reading. She may find third grade material much easier to read, will not miss quite so many words on a page at this level, and with help, she will be able to figure out most of the new words. In this case, the third grade reading material would be her *instruction level.* If Mary is able to pick up a second grade book and read it quickly and feel comfortable with it, second grade materials are her *independent level.*

The frustration level of a student needs to be determined because it is the level at which many words become barriers to reading. It measures the point at which a student may give up because the material is too difficult. Sometimes students at the frustration level will continue to struggle even though what they are being required to read is clearly above their reading level. One may inadvertently try to teach words that are more frustration-producing than instructive. When too many unfamiliar words become barriers to general understanding, students tend to develop a dislike for reading.

The instruction level for a student is most crucial for you to determine because it is the level at which you should provide instruction. At this level your student will be learning new words, as well as learning how to figure out unknown words.

Additional instructions to help you determine the three reading levels just described are given in the *Reading Assessment Booklet: Grades 2-6.*

ORAL AND SILENT READING

After a student has read orally the material for a given grade level, a series of comprehension questions is asked.

Surprisingly, there are students who learn to read without paying attention to much of what they are reading; thus their comprehension is poor. Such students are referred to as *word callers*. They can read words very well, even at a high level, but they have not learned to think about the meaning of what they read. If your students are to progress in reading, it is absolutely essential that they develop good comprehension skills.

There are many children who read aloud quite well, but when they are asked to read "to themselves," they are unable to do so. Poor comprehension in silent reading is frequently caused when a student is taught to read orally but silent reading practice is neglected. In this situation, students sometimes learn words without having to think about their meanings.

Following is an illustration of a paragraph story which has been used to diagnose reading comprehension levels, along with questions to determine comprehension:

"Louis (Satchmo) Armstrong is credited with making jazz an accepted part of American culture. Born on July 4, 1900, in New Orleans,

Louisiana, Armstrong's musical career as trumpeter and vocalist is permanently tied to the history of American jazz. Louis Armstrong took jazz out of . . . New Orleans, where it was born, and introduced it as an art form around the world. He had become a legend in his own lifetime. Wherever New Orleans jazz is played, Satchmo is known and respected as one of the greatest jazz musicians."*

*Typical Comprehension Questions:***

1. Who is the story about?_____

2. Where was he born? _____

3. What instrument did he play?_____

4. Why is he considered one of the greatest jazz musicians?_____

_____

*Reprinted by permission from *How to Diagnose Your Child's Reading Problem*, Ibid., p. 143, which was reprinted from Eldonna L. Everetts, Lyman C. Hunt, Bernard Weiss, *Time to Wonder*, p. 268, by permission of the publisher (Copyright 1973, Holt, Rinehart and Winston, Inc.)

**Ibid.

The supplementary materials for this handbook provide examination stories similar to the one above, for each level from Primer through Grade Six. (These examination stories are repeated in the *Student's Reading Test Book: Grades 2-6,* and the *Reading Assessment Booklet: Grades 2-6.*) By following the instructions in the *Reading Assessment Booklet,* you will be able to assess the comprehension levels of your students.

ASSESSING FACTORS IN POOR COMPREHENSION

Comprehension is impeded when a reader skips or adds words; repeats one or more words; uses substitutions or mispronunciations; reads reversals in pronunciation or order of words; or simply does not know a word.

In order to determine kinds of comprehension-related errors which a student will need help in correcting, a reading diagnostician asks the student to read orally. Comprehension questions (as illustrated above) are asked after the reading; also, while the student is reading aloud, the diagnostician records all errors as they are made, using symbols for each kind of error. These symbols are entered in the examiner's record book, directly on or near each word or words misread.

Following are brief discussions of each kind of reading-related error, with an example of one system of symbols you can use in assessing your student's reading skills.

Skipped Words

Omission of small words such as "a," "the," "had," or "not" is a common error; also, students may skip words they do not know. This kind of error can distort meaning of sentences and thus impede comprehension.

Skipped words are circled by the examiner. In the following passage the word "not" is circled which means it was omitted:

EXAMPLE: "I am (not) going with you."

Added Words

Poor readerss sometimes change meanings of sentences by adding words or word parts.

The examiner writes in any word or word part that is added by the student while reading.

EXAMPLE: "He used the pencil."

Repetitions

Repetitious reading behavior, while not an error *per se* , can interrupt comprehension. However, it should be recorded only when two or more words are repeated.

Repetitions are sometimes recorded by underlining with an arrow the part of a sentence that the student repeats.

EXAMPLE: "We jumped in the truck and took off."

Substitutions and Mispronunciations

A student who makes substitutions for words he or she is reading, or mispronounces them, can easily lose the meaning of what is being read. Some students will make this kind of error by attempting to sound out a word without trying to understand its meaning.

Substitutions and mispronounced words are characteristic of students who do not know how to read for meaning; they may see a word within a word, or pick up consonant blends and complete the word through guessing, without any regard for whether or not it makes sense in the sentence.

Mark substitutions and mispronunciations by crossing out the printed word that was wrongly-read and writing in the student's word.

EXAMPLE: "~~Every~~ *Very* morning, the ~~blue~~ *blow* flower opened its ~~petals.~~ *pencil*"

(NOTE: During assessment, do not correct these errors unless the student asks or waits for help; then say the word for him or her, but count the error. Repeated errors on the same word are counted as a single error.)

Reversals

Reversals in pronunciation or word order often result from carelessness in reading, from nervousness on the part of the student, or merely from his or her attempting to read rapidly.

Use the standard proofreading symbol for reversals. This is a curved line that, in proofreading, indicates a typo or change in grammar, e.g., "evidnece."

In assessing oral reading, the curved line symbol is used to show reversals made by the student.

EXAMPLE: "The rabbit saw four new animals playing."

In this example, "saw" was pronounced as "was" and "animals playing" was read as "playing animals."

Unknown Words

In tutoring situations unknown words should be supplied promptly. As the student progresses, you should make a point of sounding out the word before pronouncing it. (This is preferable to pressuring the student and will encourage him or her to follow your example.)

When measuring comprehension skills, you should give the student plenty of time to try the word, then pronounce it yourself and mark it with a minus sign over the word to show it was missed.

EXAMPLE: "I <u>asked</u> the man."

Context of Words

One important element in reading comprehension, which cannot be measured on an oral reading test, is the ability to figure out the meaning of a word from its context. For example, the word *neighbor* might be baffling to a child until he or she considers it as part of the sentence, "Our neighbor came to borrow a cup of milk."

Sentences that contain words which sound alike but have different meanings (homonyms) are useful in teaching students to watch for context. ("He asked the butcher to *meet* him on the corner with a package of *meat*;" or "Bob *ate* breakfast at *eight* o'clock.")

By the same token, words that are spelled alike but have meanings dependent on their use (homographs) also provide chances to teach the concept of context. ("She

told me to *read* over what the class had just *read* together;"
or "The oil *well* is producing *well*.")

Students usually show more interest in learning the
differences between two or more homonyms, or two or
more homographs, if they are *asked* to help construct sentences with them instead of being asked to pick them out
of prepared sentences.

9

Measuring Attack Skills

In this chapter we will discuss assessing auditory discrimination, phonetics and word recognition skills: word attack skills that can be measured and improved.

AUDITORY DISCRIMINATION

Auditory discrimination is the ability to hear differences between sounds. It is surprising how many students do not hear certain sounds correctly. However, if particular auditory discrimination failures are recognized during testing, then they can be corrected by specific remediation techniques. The following illustrates one method commonly used to test auditory discrimination.

During an initial testing session, the reading diagnostician stands behind a student and says:

"I am going to pronounce three words. Two words are alike and one is different. Tell me which word is different."

Set 1:	about	above	about
Set 2:	what	when	what
Set 3:	bound	bought	bound
Set 4:	came	came	come
Set 5:	street	stripe	stripe
Set 6:	book	look	book

By following instructions in the *Reading Assessment Booklet: Grades 2-6*, you will be able to assess the auditory discrimination skills of your students.

After proper assessment, your key to developing auditory discrimination skills—given effective treatment of any hearing impairments—is through exercises in listening, which are described in Part D of this handbook.

PHONIC SKILLS

The phonic approach to teaching reading has been a controversial subject for many years. Many educational battles have been fought over whether a child should be taught by the phonetic method or the sight (look-say) method. Our position is that both methods are necessary.

The word *phonic* means "producing sounds." In the case of reading, it means producing the sounds for each of the letters in the alphabet. Everyone needs to develop this skill in order to learn to identify words without constant help.

Some teachers drill their students over the sounds of individual letters, from a to z. Others teach phonics by having children listen carefully for beginning sounds (a for apple, b for ball, c for cat, etc.). Students can then be asked to name words they can think of that begin like apple, ball, cat, and so on through the alphabet. Thus, students are taught to listen closely to sounds, and to associate similar sounds that occur in different words. Normally, students learn phonics in first grade, but many students are not ready to master letter sounds at this level.

The materials provided in the *Reading Assessment Booklet: Grades 2-6* describe how you can determine whether or not your student knows phonics thoroughly. The materials are divided into consonants and vowels, digraphs and blends.

Vowels

Frequently, children easily master consonant sounds but have trouble with vowels. Vowels have more than one sound, occur in the middle of words, and can be "silent" in a word, so it is difficult to attach the correct sounds to them in different combinations of spelling. Thus, after elementary vowel sounds are learned, their applications to individual words are taught through practice in reading and spelling.

Digraphs

Digraphs are two consonant letters which combine to make one sound. Examples are: *sh* as in shoe, short, shop, shout, should; *th* as in thank, that, these, those, this; *wh* as in what, which, why, where; *ch* as in chance, chop, cheese, choose.

Blends

Blends are two consonants which blend together in words. Examples are: *cl* as in clap, claw, clip, class; *gl* as in glass, glare, gleam; *fr* as in free, from, frank; *st* as in street, stripe, stroke; *bl* as in blue, black, blow.

After you have assessed the phonetic skills of a student as instructed in the *Reading Assessment Booklet: Grades 2-6*, there are a number of activities you may carry out, depending on that assessment; these are described in Part D of this handbook.

WORD RECOGNITION

You will need to know at what level your student can look at words and pronounce them quickly and accurately. In this case, you *do not* want to determine the student's ability to use phonics but to pronounce whole words rapidly and correctly.

To test word recognition skills, say to the student, *"read all of the words in the first column illustrated below."* After the words in the first column have been read, proceed as far as the student can possibly go, even if many mistakes are being made. Continue until five words have been missed in succession.

The illustrative lists below are from pre-primer through first grade reading levels.

Pre Primer	Primer	First Reader
a	at	again
and	are	other
big	boy	off
can	came	be
come	did	over
father	for	know
go	he	please

Additional lists of words for pre-primer through sixth grade levels are provided in the *Reading Assessment Booklet: Grades 2-6* and the *Student's Reading Test Book: Grades 2-6.*

When assessing word recognition skills, be alert to whether or not your students stop to look at each letter as they attempt to sound out words. Also note whether or not beginning sounds are pronounced properly and whether or not ending sounds are pronounced properly.

Listen closely as your students read to see if they break words apart and sound them out. Be especially alert to whether or not they take wild guesses without looking at words carefully.

In the *Reading Assessment Booklet: Grades 2-6*, more detailed instructions are given for assessing the auditory, phonetic and word recognition skills of students.

In the next part of this handbook practical activities and ideas are presented for improving these and the other reading skills of students.

PART D

TEACHING READING SKILLS

10

Enhancing Interest

Reading exercises and drills such as those furnished with this handbook are valuable for correction of undesirable reading habits in specific areas—but are of very little use unless the student practicing them is in a receptive frame of mind. Many of your students will tend to harbor negative attitudes toward reading exercises and drills unless they understand their value or find them interesting. Following are some suggestions on making your tutoring sessions interesting and effective.

AVOID STRICT FORMALITY

The tutoring situation has several built-in advantages over typical classroom instruction, where the teacher must attend to several children at once. Working on a one-to-one basis allows closer personal relationships between tutor and pupil than is usually possible in classes of twenty or thirty students. Because you will be one on one, you will be able to have adequate discipline without insisting on formal structure. The atmosphere of your "class" is informal and open to fully individualized instruction. Thus you have abundant chances to offer student-centered teaching at its optimum potential. Insisting on strict formality and set procedures in a tutoring situation would be missing your strongest opportunities to help the student.

AVOID BEING JUDGMENTAL

Whether they show it or not, most students who have been referred for tutoring are discouraged and low in self-confidence. You can usually start each student on the road to increased self-esteem during your first session by speaking in a straightforward, casual manner and by indicating your interest in the student as a person.

After completing the diagnostic or remedial work planned for the day, follow it up with a friendly chat in which you try to draw out the student's likes and dislikes, without sounding merely inquisitive or as if you were "trying to get something for the record." If you are not judgmental and if you show genuine attention to the student's comments, he or she will tend to sense your desire to make the times you spend together as enjoyable as possible.

WHEN SUGGESTING BOOKS

While getting to know the student, you will receive clues on reading materials that will be of particular interest to him or her. Books exist on every imaginable subject, at every reading level; however, you will be wise to refrain from "pushing" reading for its own sake at the beginning.

Consider Student's Interests

Don't respond to Anthony's comment that he enjoys ice skating, or to Julie's announcement that she owns a record library, by exclaiming that you'll find books on these subjects. However, at a later session, when you show these students books from which they can make selections for oral reading, be sure that the subjects they have mentioned are well represented—at appropriate reading levels.

Beginning with your first session with each student, have on hand some easily-understood, humorous or high-interest materials from which the student can select something to read to you after the work period. These materials can include comic books, simple joke books and brief stories.

Consider Student's Reading Level

When selecting books for enjoyable reading, the student's personal interests should always be considered, and the material should be at a reading level slightly higher than the student's measured one. It is one thing to offer easy reading in the form of comics and jokes, but quite another when you are asking a student to read a story

which involves a longer attention span. It is better to ease
your students into challenging material by giving generous
help in the beginning stages than it is to let them become
bored, or insulted, by books that contain nothing but simple words.

Some students will become ambitious to read books
or magazines that have fascinating subject matter or attrac-
tive pictures, but are too difficult for them to read without
help. When one of your students brings material such as
this to you, bearing in mind that his or her interest is already high, you can expect more reading effort. Instead
of merely prompting errors, take time to write out difficult words and analyze letter sounds—perhaps even using
the tracing method discussed in Chapter 14—then include
new words that are learned in the student's word-record, as
described in that chapter.

Use Library Resources

Libraries abound with exciting and sometimes humorous stories and books* for youngsters which you can ask
students to read to you, a chapter at a time or in ten- or
fifteen-minute periods after the work session. Start this
kind of reading by 1) allowing the student to choose from

---

*See the Appendix, *Added Materials for Skills Devel-
opment by Topic and Age Levels*

two or more titles; and 2) giving copious help with reading on the first few chapters. Once you sense that the student is involved in the story and enjoying it, you can gradually eliminate prompting for errors—excepting in cases where an error has altered the meaning of the story.

AVOID OVERCORRECTING

When listening to a student read, it is advised that you restrain yourself from correcting every word missed. When a mistake changes the meaning of the material, simply point out the misread word or sentence by reading it correctly yourself. In short—don't force your students to do a lot of sounding-out in this situation, which should be kept as pleasurable as possible. As each student's interest in the material increases, he or she will read more carefully for meaning. By being casually helpful instead of insisting on allowing reading to be a laborious process, you will encourage students to relax and become less self-conscious about errors, so they can give fuller attention to what the words are saying.

SAVE TIME FOR FUN

The more actual reading practice a student gets, the faster he or she will progress. By choosing kinds of practice the student can enjoy, you may be able to engage in enjoyable instructional activities during the last fifteen or twenty minutes of each tutoring hour.

BE PATIENT

Should students show reluctance to enter into conversation with you, don't persist in questioning or talking —but *do* persist in being casually friendly. There are several activities or games you can use to fill out the remainder of each session, all of which offer reading-related diversions while providing opportunities for you to become better acquainted. Schools, libraries and childrens' magazines are good sources for such materials.

VARY ACTIVITIES

It is advisable to introduce a variety of activities until you find the student's preferences. Then, after exercises and drills have been completed, reward the student by suggesting his or her preferred activities to fill out the time you spend together.

After you have tutored several students you will develop your own methods for reaching satisfactory tutor-student relationships. However, your main thrust should be toward a consistent atmosphere of reading and student-centeredness.

TAKE TURNS READING

In any reading which has one or more difficult words to a sentence, it is a good idea to take turns with the student in reading aloud. If you read every other paragraph, the student's attention will be maintained better than if there is constant interruption for analysis of words.

HELP WITH SCHOOL WORK

You can provide homework assistance in many ways which will help students to carry new skills into the classroom.

Spelling words can be taught by the tracing method (Chapter 14), which usually brings dramatic improvement in spelling grades.

When reading science or social studies with a student, there is a specific routine you can follow that will help him or her to learn the material and at the same time develop study skills. First, look over the assignment with the student, pointing out the headings and sub-headings and discussing their meaning. Then, while the assignment is being read aloud to you, stop to explain and talk about the points that are important—pointing out how they are related to the headings and sub-headings. After the assignment has been read (with whatever amount of help is necessary from you in order for the student to understand it), go back over the main points, following headings and sub-headings and asking questions about them.

In helping with homework writing assignments, get the student to express what he wants to write but resist all temptation to do his or her work. Leave sentences as they are worded by the student, helping only with spelling if asked. If a list of questions is to be answered over a text-book assignment, help the student find the appropriate heading or sub-heading—and to read the material if help is needed—but leave phrasing of the answer to the student. Your aim is to help him or her to develop reading and study skills which will lead to independent learning.

SUMMARY

The tutoring activities described in this book, with proper execution, will enable you to help the student real-ize that reading has something to offer him or her which is not related exclusively to grades earned in the classroom. Nearly always, students who say they hate reading have developed this attitude through experiences of failure. By accepting the student as he or she is, and by building a friendly relationship, you can prove your genuine desire to share the pleasures and advantages of knowing how to read.

11

Developing
Comprehension Skills

Having students read aloud helps to keep you in touch with what they are learning. Furthermore, oral practice has certain advantages in developing comprehension.

However, too much emphasis on oral reading will encourage some students to become "word callers" who are unable to pay sufficient attention to the content of what they are reading. Therefore, practice in silent reading is also essential for interest and comprehension.

PRAISE ORAL AND SILENT READING

Children in the first and second grades sometimes find it difficult to silently read a book by themselves. However, they usually love to have parents or friends sit with them as they read aloud story after story. You should not, however, discourage oral reading. Reading, orally or silently, should be encouraged and praised. Appropriate reinforcement of oral reading will contribute to the enjoyment of reading silently—especially when you take the time to discuss the material that is being read.

SUGGESTIONS FOR READING PRACTICE

It must be emphasized that if you find it necessary to pronounce more than three or four words on a page during exercises in oral reading, you are approaching the student's frustration level. This means the material you are using is too difficult and should be set aside in favor of material more in accord with the student's instructional level.

If you go through the story yourself before presenting it to a student, you should be able to anticipate difficulty with certain words. These words might be taught to the student before he or she starts reading the book. Following is a simple example of this technique.

Suppose you intend to introduce to a young student a story that begins:

John had a brown dog.
His name was Flip.
He ran away one day.
John found him in a yard far away.

You may have previously determined that this student has difficulty with "sight" words—those which should be known from memory. In this case you would review words such as *had, his, was* and *away* with the child before starting the story. On the other hand, if you have found the youngster is well grounded on such basic words, but has trouble with sounding out new ones, you would use phonic clues to teach the words *brown, name, ran, found* and *yard.* (If it turns out the student is already familiar with words you have chosen for drill, checking them out will still serve a double purpose; it will assure you that his or her reading will be quick and accurate, and bolster his or her self-reliance in tackling the material.)

You will be surprised at the confidence a student develops after becoming able to read an entire page without help. Prior word practice will also help the student avoid being forced to labor over individual words.

FOCUS ON CONTENT

Comprehension skills are developed by paying attention to the content of what is being read, on a systematic basis. Before starting either oral or silent reading practice, you can catch the student's interest by telling him or her something about the story—just enough to arouse curiosity.

Recall

After the reading is completed, say, "Now tell me about what you have read." It is wise to try to get the student in the habit of recalling details without a great deal of prompting. Once a student has told you what he or she has remembered, you might ask one or two questions. It is important to stress meanings; after all, what words communicate is the purpose of reading.

Order of Events

There are students who have a tendency to get the order of events in a story confused, who will retell what they have just read by starting at the ending or at midpoint, or will transpose the order of events in some other way. If a student does this, review the story by asking, "What happened first?" And help him or her to recall the correct train of events with questions *indicating your interest in the story rather than an obvious attempt to force "right answers."*

However, if this method of review fails to help the student remember a story in logical order, you might present a series of questions that follow the story line This will serve as a model for development of orderly memory.

Questions for Full Comprehension

The series-of-questions approach is valuable in teaching full comprehension as well as orderly memory.

After the student reads:

John had a brown dog.
His name was Flip.
He ran away one day.
John found him in a yard far away,

you might immediately ask, "What did John have?" "What was his name?" "What did the dog do?" "Did John find him?"

Thought Questions

These very simple questions will be easily answered by most students. You can then proceed to a few "thought" questions such as, "Why do you suppose John named his dog Flip?" "Why do you think the dog ran away?" "What do you think John did when he found his dog?" "Do you think he was happy?"

Questions such as this, *posed with a genuine show of interest in the student's response*, serve to help the reader become involved in the story and are invaluable aids to comprehension—which is dependent on interest above all else.

In case you are working with a third grader and using first grade level materials, you may not have to be overly concerned with comprehension; nevertheless, the content of whatever has been read must be discussed to help the student read for meaning at all times.

FURTHER DEVELOPMENT
OF COMPREHENSION SKILLS

Following is a list of suggestions to aid you in assisting students to better understand what they read.

1. Ask open-ended questions during the reading such as, "What do you think will happen next?" Follow up later with "Were you right?"

2. Have the student read to find out *why*.

3. Read until the student can tell you about one certain incident, mentioned ahead of time.

4. Ask for a prediction of what might happen at the end of a story.

5. Assure the students, particularly young students, that reading is "talk written down" and that the words are merely words we all use every day; therefore, reading always "tells" the reader something.

6. Stress that reading is *thinking*.

The beginning of a lesson for a younger student might go as follows: say, "Look at the pictures on the page. What do you think is happening?" "How do the characters feel?" "Can you tell by their faces the kind of mood they are in?"

Concept Development

You can also call attention to concepts with questions such as, "What time of day is it in the picture?" "Is that an ocean or a river?" "Is this a city or farm story?"

You do not always need to test comprehension. The idea is to arouse interest, which will automatically develop comprehension skills. It is important to build students' awareness that *reading is thinking*.

Comprehending From Context

Comprehension is often aided by learning to recognize a word from the meaning of the rest of the sentence. Here is a sample exercise that can be used to develop sentence meaning through the use of context clues:

Rabbits live in _____ .
houses   woods   trees   streets

It is hot in the _____ .
winter   summer

Bears like _____ .
honey   bees

At other times, a word can be identified from the contents of a picture illustrating the story; for example, if

the book is about John in an airplane, the student will
tend to pick up context clues for the word "airplane"
from the picture.

Using Pictures

Pictures and photographs can be used to develop
comprehension of abstract concepts such as love, anger,
friendship, sadness and happiness. Plentiful illustrations of
abstract meanings can be found in magazines, newspapers
and books. Discussion of these concepts can help you learn
a great deal about a student's self-concept as well as his or
her feelings concerning school, friends, home and the rest
of the world.

COMPREHENSION OF VERBAL DIRECTIONS

Many students are unable to follow more than one
verbal direction at a time. While this may not at first glance
seem relevant to reading comprehension, it is basic to all
understanding of, and memory for, words and their meanings. A common complaint of teachers and parents is voic-
ed in the familiar sentence, "If you had listened to what I
said, you'd have known what to do next."

Rather than becoming increasingly exasperated with a
student who fails to follow a sequence of directions, you

can turn it into a game that will challenge the student and lend pleasure to his or her learning. Begin with simple requests, and add to the number of directions gradually. This game is described in detail under *Exercise Games* in Chapter 12.

12

Developing
Listening Skills

Should a student have difficulty differentiating sounds, it will be wise to spend time developing auditory skills at the beginning of your instruction. Sometimes a student's inability to sound out words is caused by a lack of knowing the sounds and how to distinguish between sounds as they are spoken.

DISTINGUISHING BETWEEN SOUNDS

Teaching sound discrimination should be along the same lines as the test that measures auditory performance. First of all, say two words, then ask the student to tell you if you said the same word or different words. Following are some words you can use. You will undoubtedly wish to add others after you have identified the student's individual trouble-spots in this area. You will note that this list includes some pairs of words that are identical.

ball - bat	what - where
bean - been	why - why
big - dog	shall - shell
cat - come	be - big
was - saw	crab - crib
this - them	gang - gang
that - that	here - where

Should you discover that a student does not pay attention to ending sounds, give groups of words with similar and different ending sounds.

cat - cook	dog - dot	flat - flop
hot - hook	drip - drill	got - gone
bat - ball	ear - eat	run - rut
blue - blue	fat - far	sat - sap

As you work on auditory skills, you may discover that your student is able to hear the sounds accurately, but merely has been inattentive to previous instruction.

BE A GOOD LISTENER YOURSELF

The most effective way to teach listening skills is to be a good listener yourself. When students talk to you, look into their eyes and give them your individual attention. Do not interrupt. Listen to all they have to say, then ask questions and listen to the answers. One frequent mistake adults make is to talk *at* students instead of *with* them.

EXERCISES AND GAMES

Most classroom teachers have developed many techniques for teaching students to listen. Effective teachers recognize that in order to teach students, they must be able to hold their attention.

Simon Says

The game "Simon Says" is one that many of us played as children. It is a particularly good one for teaching listening skills, even to older students, in group sessions.

The person who is "it" issues directions, as rapidly as possible, for the others to follow, either using or omitting the words "Simon says" as a gimmick to trap his listeners into making a mistake. For example, when the person who is "it" declares, "Simon says thumbs up!" everyone is supposed to put thumbs up; but if the command is simply "Thumbs up!" or "Thumbs down!" anyone who follows it must drop out of the game (or—if only two are playing—must take the part of "it"). Additional short commands (not longer than two or three words) such as "Stand up!" "Sit down!," "Close your eyes!," and "Laugh!" or "Cry!"

may be used to make the game more complicated for older children. The main thrust of the exercise is rapid delivery of commands, which forces careful attention to listening.

Eyes Closed

Both you and your student close your eyes, then try to identify everything you can hear. Let your student start naming sounds, then add to the list with additional ones he or she has missed. (Someone is hammering, cars are passing by, a pencil is being tapped, a horn is blowing, or a bird is chirping.) Let the student compete with you in listening for more detailed discrimination, such as determining whether a vehicle going by is a car or a truck, what kind of bird might be chirping, or even who might be doing the hammering.

Moon Trip

Another favorite game starts with the person playing "it" stating, "I am going to the moon and I am going to take along something that begins with ___," filling the blank with a letter from the alphabet. As the game proceeds from one player to the next, each player names all the words beginning with that letter which have already been called, and then adds a new word. This game can be varied by starting with a word from the leader that begins with "a" and requiring successive players to call out words beginning with successive letters of the alphabet, in exact

order, after repeating each word that has already been called. (Example: apple, ball, cat, dog, elephant—and on
through the alphabet.) Any players failing to recall all
words in proper sequence would drop out until the winner
(or the one who remembers most) is left, to become "it"
for the next round.

Playing Rhythms

This is a game that not only teaches a student to listen, but in addition helps him or her to categorize objects
and to follow directions. Tap your knees, clap your hands,
then snap your fingers and say a category of objects, such
as states, cars, flowers, fruits, or cities. The aim is to keep a
rhythm going by first one person saying an object in the
category, then the next player using the same rhythm and
saying another object in that category.

For example, suppose "states" is the category chosen
by the first player. This person would call out the word
"states," while demonstrating a basic rhythm he or she has
selected. Suppose the basic rhythm in this case involves
two foot taps followed by two hand claps. The second
player would be expected to name a state while tapping his
or her foot twice, then clapping hands twice. In turn, the
third player names a third state while reproducing the
same rhythm pattern. Each player who fails to name a
state not yet called, or who breaks the rhythmic routine,
drops out, until a single player survives as "winner."

Following Directions Game

To give a student practice in listening to directions and following them properly, you might play a game such as the following:

1. Start by saying "Hand me the book."

2. After the command is followed, say "Hand be the book and close the door."

3. Then, add another item to each command in succession, "Hand me the book, close the door, and put an "x" on the paper."

4. "Hand me the book, close the door, put an "x" on the paper, and jump three times."

5. "Hand me the book, close the door, put an "x" on the paper, jump three times, and turn to page 20."

See how far the student can go, but remember to make it a game.

Leaving-Out-A-Word

Say a complete sentence such as, "Father went to the store to buy a hammer, nails, and a saw." Now repeat the sentence and leave out a word. The object is to have your student recall the word you omitted. "Father went to the ____to buy a hammer, nails, and a saw." Build sentences yourself and see how complicated you can make them. Students love this game, which can be varied by reversing rules and letting them make up the sentences with missing words for you to guess.

"I am thinking of . . . " Game

Begin by saying, "I am thinking of a word that begins like cat." Any word response that begins with the same sound is correct even though the word might begin with a "k." Repeat the process, using other beginning sounds; then switch to ending sounds, then to middle sounds.

Rhyming

Youngsters love rhyming, and will invariably respond to games that include it. A simple game of rhyming single words provides excellent listening practice.

Say "I am thinking of a word that rhymes with *bear*. Can you guess the word?"

Limit the number of guesses to four or five. If the student fails to suggest words that rhyme with the one you have named, illustrate by pronouncing several that do and tell him or her the one you had in mind.

Once the student understands the concept of rhyming you could vary the game by thinking up actual rhymes. Example: "The hungry bear tried to eat a chair."

Another variation would be to ask questions such as:

1. You write with it and it sounds like stencil. What is it?

2. It is red and sounds like nose. What is it?

3. You read it and it sounds like look. What is it?

4. It is a brown animal and sounds like hair. What is it?

13

Developing
Phonic Skills

Most students who are old enough for special tutoring have been exposed to phonics since their reading readiness training in kindergarten. However, some youngsters become confused by beginning phonics. In classroom stiuations students can fake knowledge of letter sounds, especially when phonics exercises are done in chorus, or stumble through oral reading at higher levels without revealing their confusion over certain letter sounds.

Your preliminary testing should pinpoint the individual letters a student needs to work on, so it should not be necessary to review every letter with him or her. Many of your students will have other kinds of reading problems—a few of them will even to over-exposed to phonics and consequently need help with whole word-recognition and sentence-reading—not phonics.

In any case, phonics exercises should be kept separate from regular oral reading. When a student stumbles over a word while reading to you, don't say, "sound it out."

Simply pronounce it to prevent interruption of comprehension, then go through the sounding-out process with
the student later.

In addition, phonics drills must be kept brief, since
they quickly grow tedious. It is better to teach phonics as
an incidental sideline activity. Limit your phonics activities
to no more than one exercise per day and no longer than
ten minutes of phonics instruction in one session.

This chapter discusses letter sounds in detail and includes some illustrative phonics games and exercises that
can be used with younger students. For your convenience
in referring to exercises needed by individual students, the
chapter includes instruction on:

1. Consonants

   a. beginning and ending sounds
   b. digraph and blend sounds

2. Vowels

   a. short and long sounds
   b. vowel combinations

3. Some general principles for pronunciation and
   meaning

4. Building words

When working with phonics, use a felt tip pen and a pad of paper; or a small chalkboard that can be used on your desk or table. This can be used to keep track of words missed during oral reading, for practice with individual letters and for word-building exercises.

CONSONANTS

Beginning Sounds

There are many simple alphabet cards and books on the market that teach beginning and ending sounds. For example, *The Sesame Street Book of Letters* teaches each beginning sound with a jingle and also shows where the letter fits into the alphabet. In teaching the letter "h," the jingle goes, "Is Happy Harry Hidden in His Hole?" This process is repeated with each letter.

Using this type of material to teach beginning sounds is certainly a lot more enjoyable than isolating sounds which have no connection with actual words.

Illustrative Exercise 1

Teaching letter sounds by attaching them to words makes them more meaningful. You could start with beginning consonants by asking the student to think of words beginning with "b" and writing them on your pad or chalkboard, underlining the first letter each time. For example, say, "Now we are going to learn the sound of "b"" (immediately repeat the phrase *"sound of b"* twice, emphasizing the word "sound" in the phrase). Then write "b̲oy," "b̲all," etc.

Stick with beginning sounds at this point. Do not ask the student to spell or write the words—you write each word, underlining the beginning consonant sound. If necessary, this procedure can be used with every consonant.

Illustrative Exercise 2

All students are familiar with exercises that require matching beginning letters to pictures. Younger students might enjoy watching you create such exercises. Draw one column of pictures and another column of consonant letters. A key to this is having easily recognized pictures. Have the student draw the connecting lines as in this example.

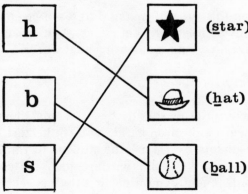

Illustrative Exercise 3

Another exercise involves asking the student to draw circles around words that begin with the same sound, using a list like the one that follows, and phrasing your instructions like this: "Draw circles around the words that begin the same as *cat* and *come*," (or *dig* and *doll, sing* and *so,* etc.)

dog	big	bat	run
cry	came	sat	bite
boat	boy	can	coat

Use exercises such as the above only when a student's problems with letters warrants it—and remember to keep the time periods brief. Whenever possible, use words in the exercises that the student is already working with in another reading task.

Ending Sounds

Ending consonant sounds are taught in the same way as beginning ones, by looking at them in words, writing them down and underlining the last letter. The above exercises can be modified to accommodate ending sounds. For example, the above exercises can be modified as follows:

Illustrative Exercise 1

Draw one column of ending consonant letters and another column of pictures of objects which illustrate the ending consonant. Have the student draw connecting lines, as illustrated.

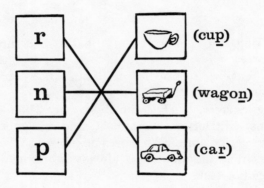

Illustrative Exercise 2

Present the student with two columns of words which can be matched by their ending sounds. Have the student draw a line matching the words, as illustrated below:

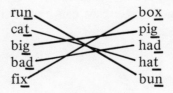

Illustrative Exercise 3

The latter exercise can be carried a step further, after both beginning and ending sounds have been practiced, by use of words that have the same beginning *and* ending consonants. Have the student draw lines connecting as shown in the following illustration:

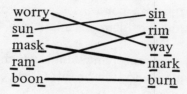

Illustrative Exercise 4

The two consonants which appear most confusing to readers are *b* and *d* because these letters exactly reverse one another.

To impress both the shapes and sounds of these letters, print the word *bed*. Draw a light line over the *e* (between *b* and *d*) to produce a rough picture of a bed, with the headboard and footboard represented by the two letters.

b e̅ d

This presents an association to which the student can always refer whenever he is having trouble remembering the name of either letter or its sound.

Digraph and Blend Sounds

There are four digraph sounds you may need to work on. These digraphs are combinations of consonants that produce *one* sound. The digraphs are th, wh, ch, and sh.

Blends are *two* consonant sounds which blend together. The consonant blends are br, bl, pl, st, cl, cr, dr, fl, fr, gr, sc, sk, sm, sn, sp, st, and tr.

Illustrative Exercise 1

If you have purchased a set of word cards in which you match the sound with a picture, the publishers may have also included the digraphs and blends, as illustrated on the following page.

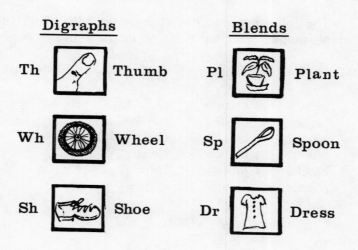

If they haven't, see how creative you can be. Make your own.

Illustrative Exercise 2

After blends and digraphs have been taught, the student can practice distinguishing between the two. You might play the following game by first stating, "The word *blue* begins like *black, blink* and *blond*. Can you think of any other words that begin like *blue* and *blink*?" (Illustrative answers are *block, blank*, and *bloom.)*

The following are illustrative words with blend and digraph sounds you may teach as in the above example:

bl	br	ch	cl
blue	brain	chair	clam
black	braid	cheek	clamp
blow	break	cherry	class
bloom	branch	chest	clear
block	brave	chill	cliff
blond	breath	chimney	cloud

cr	dr	fl	fr
crab	draw	flag	frame
cradle	drink	flame	free
crack	drain	flair	freeze
crew	drive	flash	friend
crate	drill	floor	front
cream	drop	flower	frost

gl	gr	pl	pr
glass	grade	plain	practice
glider	grain	plan	praise
globe	grand	place	pray
glue	grape	plank	print
glossy	green	plow	price
glory	grow	plus	prize

s̲c̲	s̲h̲	s̲k̲	s̲l̲
scale	shade	skip	slam
score	shake	ski	slap
scar	sharp	skin	sleep
scare	shave	skirt	slow
scrap	shark	sky	slip
scream	shop	skunk	slug

s̲m̲	s̲n̲	s̲p̲	s̲t̲
small	snake	spade	stable
smart	snap	spark	stage
smell	snow	spare	stamp
smile	snore	spank	star
smoke	snag	spot	step
smooth	sneak	spider	storm

s̲w̲	t̲h̲	t̲r̲	t̲w̲
swallow	think	trace	twelve
swap	that	tractor	twenty
swear	there	trade	twin
swell	thin	trap	twig
swing	those	tree	twinkle
swift	thumb	trunk	twist

<u>wh</u>	<u>wr</u>
whale	wreck
wheat	wrist
wheel	wrong
whip	wrap
whisper	wrench
white	wrinkle

VOWELS

Teaching vowel sounds and their rules may be your most difficult and tedious task, but if you prepare your lesson ahead of time and know just what material and procedures you will use, you can ease the process. As stated before, you should work on drills of this kind only a short time during the reading session. There are many helpful materials on the market today. You may find out what is available at school by checking with the student's teacher or, if you are in private practice, at a local bookstore.

Start teaching vowel sounds with your paper and felt pen; you should be doing all of the writing at this point, unless the student shows eagerness to write. The less pressure you exert, the easier it will be to hold attention.

Short and Long Sounds

First of all, find out whether or not the student is familiar with the two short sounds made by *a* as: 1) when *a* is followed by most consonants as in *man, mat, bag, can, cat,* etc.; and 2) when *a* is followed by *r* as in *mar, bar,* and *car,* or by *ll* as in *call, ball,* and *tall.* Like the other vowels, the letter *a* also has one long sound—as in *cake, mate* and *rate.*

Illustrative Exercise 1

The short *a* sound as in *bat* can be taught by asking the student to tell you any words he or she can think of which have this short *a* sound and you write them down, indicating approval of each correct response. At first, the student will probably give you words that rhyme, such as *mat* or *sat* to go with your prompting word of *bat.* You may need to prompt with other words that end in different letters. If the student wants to write the words, permit him or her to do so.

Illustrative Exercise 2

You may repeat *Exercise 1* above to teach the other short *a* sound, as sounded in *car* or *ball.*

Illustrative Exercise 3

You can help students to identify most long *a* sounds by demonstrating that addition of the final (silent) *e* will change both the sound of the vowel and the meaning of the word.

mat (e)	mad (e)	Sam (e)	rat (e)
can (e)	car (e)	bar (e)	mar (e)

Complete the teaching of long *a* sounds with words which demonstrate that when *a* is followed by *i*, the *i* is silent: *sail, pail, nail, paint, bait, wail,* etc.

The same kinds of exercises can be used to teach the rest of the vowels. As you proceed, you can point out that when *e* is followed by *a*, the *a* is usually silent: *eat, bean, ear, jeans,* etc.; when *o* is followed by *a*, it is usually silent: *boat, coal, foam, roast,* etc.

Vowel Combinations

The various vowel combinations present many problems because rules designed to cover them do not apply consistently.

Probably the best way to teach the main vowel combinations is to make word lists containing them. However, not much time should be spent at this, as most students gain knowledge in this area rather rapidly through spelling and reading, after fundamental letter sounds have been mastered. Sample lists showing some vowel combinations follow:

List 1	List 2	List 3	List 4	List 5
foil	zoom	mouse	gaudy	piece
join	spool	around	Maude	field
point	goon	loud	sauna	priest

SOME GENERAL PRINCIPLES
FOR PRONUNCIATION AND MEANING

No phonics rules should be taught before they have been illustrated repeatedly. In this section, general principles already covered are restated, and a few others are added.

1. When a word contains two vowels, one of which is final *e*, the first vowel is usually long and the final *e* is silent.

2. When two vowels come together in a word, the first vowel generally has the long sound and the second vowel is often silent.

3. *k* followed by *n* at the beginning of a word is silent.

4.　　The letters *q* and *u* always appear together and are sounded *kw.*

5.　　When *c* or *g* is followed by *e, i* or *y,* it usually has the soft sound. *(ceiling, decide, cypress, gentleman, image, energy)*

6.　　The word *here* is in *there* and *where*—and the word *hear* has *ear* in it.

7.　　*ph* has the sound of *f* as in *elephant* and *telephone.*

8.　　*gh* has the sound of *f*—but is sometimes silent. Teach the student to write this sentence: "The rou*gh* lad thou*gh*t he threw the ball throu*gh* the window." The sentence also helps students to distinguish between *thought* and *through.*

BUILDING WORDS*

Students learn easily that letters represent sounds, and that combinations of letters form words. To broaden

---

*This section is adapted by permission of the authors, Doris B. Mosier and Ruth B. Park from *Teacher-Therapist, A Handbook for Teachers of Emotionally Impaired Children,* Chapter 9 (publication in process).

their understanding of the reading process, remind them that *words* stand for thoughts, images and things. It follows that when words are *written*, they still symbolize their meanings—but only when someone *reads* them and translates them back into thoughts, images and things. By asking sutdents to name words from their own vocabularies, then showing them what the words look like in writing, then asking them to read those words, you can dispel some of the fear and mystery with which many reluctant readers regard the printed page.

The idea is so basic that it is often overlooked by adults, particularly those who learned reading and writing easily as children. If you tutor in a public school, some of your students will come from homes where very little reading is done, where noboby has ever read aloud to them and in fact no children's books are to be found. Semiliteracy, actual illiteracy, and scant exposure to the English language are in the backgrounds of many children who experience school difficulties. Their early reading failures, plus the realization that they are falling farther and farther behind their classmates, tend to generate emotional reactions that compound their academic problems.

One interest-arousing game, which in most cases is new to the student, involves teaching him or her to read difficult words that are already a part of the student's vocabulary—by teaching him or her to write the word. This activity is especially successful with very poor readers who tend to reject conventional oral practice, because it builds up their confidence rapidly. Since the method appears to contain an element of magic which usually brings dramatic results, most students respond well to it.

To introduce this activity, promise the student that you will teach him or her any word he or she wants to learn, preferably the most difficult one the student can call to mind. Write the word on a chalkboard using script or printing, depending on the student's writing level, as large as the board will accommodate. Then ask the student to trace the word, using either the forefinger of the student's writing hand or the chalk, and to *say* the sound of each letter while tracing. Letters must never be pronounced, but always *sounded out* with sounding omitted for silent letters. This process is repeated as many times as the student considers necessary to learn the word. Then the board is turned face down and the student reproduces the word with pencil and paper. In case of an error, the student retraces until ready to try again. You will find that nearly every student, on first being introduced to this game, will rise to your challenge by naming a word he or she considers impossible to learn, and will then proceed to learn it quite easily. If a "too-simple" word is given, solemnly write it out and have the student trace it as a means of allaying his or her suspicions. but continue to request that "hard" words be supplied.

The game recognizes the intimate relationship between writing and reading. Any word one can write properly, one can also read. By using a method to teach spelling which employs "sounding-out" letters as they are written, you can give students practice at learning letter sounds which could be carried over to all their reading activities.

Using this method, one may teach words to poor readers of all ages, basing lessons on words supplied by the student. From word lists, the tutor can move to having the student write his or her own sentences, then letters to friends and stories about their favorite concerns, with each "new" word being learned by tracing-and-pronouncing.

Sometimes a student will aspire to master the name of every automobile manufactured, or of all kinds of animal species. But no matter how narrow the student's interest, every word requested becomes a learning tool.

It is advisable to keep a record of all words the student learns. Each word should be typed or printed on a file card for the student to file alphabetically, or printed in a notebook that has been divided in alphabetical order. This brings about incidental learning of dictionary skills and enables the student to look up words from time to time.

14

Developing Recognition Skills

Teaching word recognition skills involves:

1. using the phonic skills previously taught;

2. teaching "word families;"

3. using larger units of sounds (syllables);

4. correcting reversal and other sight-reading problems;

5. teaching meanings of words;

6. using the dictionary;

7. using *context clues*;

8, developing a sight vocabulary; and

9. some rules to help sound out words.

USING PHONIC SKILLS PREVIOUSLY TAUGHT

Knowing correct letter sounds will enable a student to sound out new words. For example, when a student sees the word "hat" in a story, he or she will remember the "h," "a" and "t" sounds from other words. Identifying the word "hat" becomes easy because individual letter sounds have been mastered. But reading is not so easy when one must continually stop and repeat the process of letter-sounding.

One of the difficulties in teaching students to break words apart for "sounding out" is that they may become what is termed overanalytical, stopping to analyze each letter as they read, even though most of the words have already been thoroughly mastered. Students who have had too much drill on letter sounds and word parts may fall into such a habit. Thus it is best to use a wide variety of approaches to reading.

It is advisable to work on word recognition separately from oral reading practice. Do not get your students into a continuous habit of sounding out words while reading. If he or she asks for help with a given word, pronounce the entire word immediately. If you say "sound it out," reading will become boring to your student and comprehension will tend to suffer.

Also, there are students who become adept at breaking words apart, but cannot combine the separate sounds to pronounce the whole word. For example, if a child sees the word "hat," he or she might say "h" - "a" - "t," but be unable to blend the three sounds together into the word. If your student reads like this, *do not dwell on individual letter sounds*, as drill on words as whole units is the approach he or she needs.

Using flash cards will help a student look at the whole word quickly. You must remember, however, that flash cards can be made into a stimulating game—or they can be extremely boring—depending on how they are used.

On individual cards, write a set of words the student should already know. These may be words that the student has been "sounding out" on each encounter. For example, you might write:

this	come	home	put
that	dog	jump	run
what	eat	keep	sat
cat	fun	look	turn
apple	fast	man	van
ball	gone	not	where

Now say, "I am going to quickly show you a word. You tell me what the word is." If an incorrect word is called, say, "no, it is____." Then proceed to the next word. *Do not* ask the student to sound it out!

TEACHING WORD FAMILIES

Students master word identification skills by learning word parts of "word families." The following exercises will help in teaching word parts.

Write the word *at*. Now write consonants before *at* to make new words. (at - *h*at, *b*at, *c*at, *s*at, *r*at, *f*at, *m*at, *p*at, *v*at.)

Write the word *an*. Write consonants before *an* to make new words. (an - *b*an, *c*an, *f*an, *m*an, *p*an, *t*an, *v*an.)

Write the word *and*. Write consonants before *and* to make new words. (and - *b*and, *h*and, *l*and, *s*and.)

Write the word *it*. Write consonants before *it* to make new words. (it - *b*it, *f*it, *h*it, *p*it, *s*it.)

TEACHING SOUND UNITS (SYLLABLES)

To teach additional word parts, use an easy dictionary, preferably one written for children. Show the student how words are divided in the dictionary.

Teach the word "syllable" and its definition: *a syllable is a whole sound within a word.* Using the dictionary, show your students how words are divided into syllables. (Examples: microscope is mi·cro·scope; recognize is rec·og·nize; airplane is air·plane.) Big, pan, sad, cat, land, sun, sit, hat, etc. are obviously all one-syllable words.

CORRECTING REVERSAL AND OTHER SIGHT-READING PROBLEMS

Some students tend to reverse the beginning and ending sounds of short words. Reversing the order of letters is usually not considered a problem until the third grade.

This type of reading difficulty may have been caused by too much emphasis on ending sounds. The student will look at the ending sound first, then perhaps the middle or the beginning. Some students may not have received instruction on the correct procedure for looking at words, so would habitually begin word identification by moving from right to left instead of left to right.

Correcting this type of problem isn't too difficult. Some of the exercises you might try are:

1.   Have the student trace the word, pronounce it sound-by-sound, and spell it as he or she traces. This may be done with a pen, sandpaper words, or in sand. You should present the word first, then have the student go over it.

2.   Do not dwell on word endings. For example, if your are going to teach a student to sound out the word

"cat," present the "t" sound by relating it to beginning sounds in words such as Tom, talk, took, together, and telephone.

3.   Don't dwell on middle sounds or beginning sounds. This causes students to focus on only one part of the word. For example, if the student does not pay attention to beginning sounds, errors such as saying "his" for "this," "all" for "fall," etc. could be made. If errors are made in the middle of words, the child may be looking at the beginning and ending sounds and neglecting the middle ones.

Another exercise to use for the student who looks at the beginning sounds and then takes a guess at the rest of the word, follows.

Put in the first letter of the desired word, so your student will be forced to look at middle and endings of all of the choices.

1.   The man put on a h_____ .
                              hit   her   hat

2.   Children w_____ at school.
                  play   work   sleep

3.   Let's play b_____ .
                  catch   ball   marbles

4. Br_____ me the book.
        Bring Give Hand

5. John st_____ out.
        was struck fell

6. Mary likes to pl _____ ball.
        play ran watch

7. Mother cooks with a p_____ .
        pan put pen

8. T_____ we will go.
    Take Tomorrow Someday

TEACHING MEANINGS OF WORDS

A student must learn that words have meanings. There are students who have developed such good phonic skills that they make guesses based on one aspect of the shape of a word, without regard for meaning. Such students might read the word "way" as "wiz," "lip" as "leep," "finger" as "finer," etc.

A student who looks at a sentence such as, "A dog had *spots* on his *back*," and reads it, "A dog had *stops* on his *book*" has learned to read by taking a quick glance at the words without letting their meanings register in his or her mind. If there is a picture of a dog on the page, the student should be guided to look at it and tell about the dog. Ask, "What does the dog have on his back?"

We have on occasion seen students who will pick up a book and begin reading it rapidly without paying attention to any of the words. For example, a sentence such as, "A dog had spots on his back," might be read, "A girl went to the store."

As you work with a student, make sure you introduce new words by stressing their meaning as well as their sounds.

USING THE DICTIONARY

To help learn meanings of words, use your dictionary to discover together the enjoyment of learning all the meanings a word might have. Youngsters are often surprised to discover the variety of definitions a word can have, as illustrated by the following examples:

Safe is:
      a place to keep articles;
      freed from harm or risk; unhurt;
      successful in making a base in baseball;
      healthy; sound;
      cautious.

Love is:
    affection based on admiration;
    warm attachment;
    enthusiasm; devotion;
    a score of zero in tennis.

Band is:
    something that binds;
    a formal promise;
    a strip to hold things together;
    a cord across the backbone of a book;
    a ring of elastic;
    a strip of grooves on a phonograph record;
    to attach oneself to a group;
    to gather together.

USING CONTEXT CLUES

Students learn to identify words through the use of *context clues*. This means that if an entire sentence is read, the meaning of a particular word may be derived from the meaning of other words in the sentence.

Your student might see a sentence such as, "Bears like to eat *honey*." If the word *honey* is not immediately known, the rest of the sentence should have given a clue as to the meaning of the word.

The following is a group of sentences to use in teaching a student to use context clues. If there are two unknown words in a sentence, pronounce one of them yourself.

1.   We buy toys and books in *stores.*

2.   Boys and girls like to *read* books.

3.   Mother baked *cakes* and *cookies.*

4.   Dad likes to catch *fish* in the lake.

5.   John took his ball and mitt to the *baseball game.*

6.   We flew in an *airplane* on our trip.

7.   A horse is a fast *animal.*

8.   In our garden we have *tomatoes, carrots,* and *lettuce.*

9.   John wants to be a *ghost* on *Halloween.*

DEVELOPING A SIGHT VOCABULARY

Emphasize to your students that certain words should be memorized, or known by "sight." These words frequently present problems and will need repetition before they are a permanent part of their reading vocabulary. Students have trouble with these words because it is difficult to attach meanings to them.

"Sight" words are part of every person's speaking vocabulary. Many of them are common prepositions and verb forms. Following are examples of sight words a student will encounter in reading:

about	must	is	not
around	like	it	your
and	the	to	when
at	of	which	this
before	off	should	that
between	in	want	these
but	at	be	those
come	will	not	got
what	able	some	have
where	for	him	said
why	once	her	here
whose	has	been	are
was	behind	again	soon
with	ask	had	give

Some reading teachers believe that students should memorize long lists of basic sight words. We do not feel this is necessary. If you find that particular words give a student trouble, write them on individual cards. Develop a card file of troublesome words. As you begin a new reading session, review the words on the cards.

Illustrative Exercise 1

The following exercise is an example of introducing basic sight words. Take a sentence such as, "Joe and Jane are here." The three basic sight words that should be known are *and, are,* and *here.* Before you have a student read the sentence, say, "There are three special short words in the next sentence which need to be learned by heart because they come up over and over in everything we read. These words are *and, are,* and *here.* Let's write each of them on separate cards, so we can remember them when we see them again."

Illustrative Exercise 2

Another useful activity is to write sentences, leaving a blank space for sight words. Encourage your students to say an appropriate word, then write it in the blank. (It is not necessary to have them write the word at this point, unless you are sure they can spell it.)

Sentences you might use for this exercise are as follows. Select a word from the list of sight words presented on the preceding page, or write the words on cards and have your student choose the appropriate word among them. The words presented below the sentences are possible words to use.

1. He ran _____ the house.
                around   behind   into

2. I will see you _____ .
                      again   soon

3. I will_____ you something.
            ask   show   give

4. John_____ Billy can play.
            and

5. Billy_____ home.
          came   went   ran

6. I shall _____ you a ball.
              give   buy   bring

7. Billy_____ two balls.
            has   had   will have

8. _____ is it?
      What   Where   When   Who

9. Mary came_____ me.
                  with

10. Billy_____here.
          was

Make up other sentences if your student needs additional practice with sight words.

As you develop a card file of sight-vocabulary words, you will be able to use it in a variety of games.

Illustrative Exercise 3

Play "concentration." Prepare two identical decks of cards. Each card in a deck should have a word printed on it that you are attempting to teach. Go through one deck reading aloud each word. Show the two decks to the student. Point out that each deck is alike. Shuffle the decks together to make one deck. Tell the student the two of you are going to play "concentration." Turn over the combined deck and spread the cards out in four rows face down. The object is to turn over one card and then turn over its matching card. If a matching card is not turned up, turn both back down and the other player is given a turn.

Reward each word remembered with a comment or brief praise, and keep a tally of the number of words remembered. At the end of the exercise add the total and say, "You remembered____words today! That's good!"

Other Exercises

If words like *what, where, when, why, this, that, these* and *those* present particular difficulties, make up

your own games to play, or use sentences such as the following. (Such words are probably the hardest words in the
English language for young students to remember.)

1. *What* is *that*?

2. I'll keep *these* and you take *those*.

3. I'll take *this* one and you take *that* one.

4. *Where* oh *where* has my little dog gone?

5. *Why* did he go *there*?

6. *When* will he come *here*?

One last word of caution: *do not have your students
attempt to sound out* basic sight words.

If your student is going to be successful at reading, he
or she must build up a large sight vocabulary—not just the
small basic sight words, but as many words as possible. The
importance of learning all of the word recognition techniques is to be able to look at a word quickly and identify
it without relying on any one method for identification.
When adults read they rarely think about letter sounds.

Even when a difficult word is encountered, a practiced reader will look at the entire word and not at its
parts. Also, silent reading demands comprehension—not
pronunciation. Students who stop to sound out each word

tend to use lip movements while they are reading silently; this habit slows oral reading speed while it adds nothing to comprehension.

SOME RULES TO HELP SOUND OUT WORDS

Once your student has mastered the consonant and vowel sounds, and is beginning to master word recognition techniques, it will be wise to teach a few rules which should be of additional help in reading.

Endings Added to Words (ly, ed, ing, er, y)

1. Write the word *sad*.

2. If you want to write *sadder*, double the consonant "d" before adding *er*.

3. The rule that applies here is:

    When you have a one-syllable word with a final consonant and one vowel before it, the final consonant is doubled before adding an ending (er, est, ing, ed, y, etc.). *The final consonant must be heard.* For example, in the word "blowing," the "w" is not sounded; thus it is not doubled.

4.   Now for some practice.

a.   What endings have been added to the following words:

sit*ting*	bat*ter*
bil*ling*	trip*ping*
sad*der*	hot*ter*
fit*ting*	sip*ping*

b.   Write some words and let your student add appropriate endings.

Two Consonant Sounds at the End

When a word has *two* consonant sounds at the end, the final consonant is *not* doubled.

1.   In the following words there are two consonants at the end of the words, therefore the final consonants are not doubled:

back*ing*	rest*ing*
cart*ed*	wish*ing*
sing*er*	coach*ing*
pick*ing*	cold*er*
pack*ing*	cast*ing*
fly*ing*	bang*ing*

2.   Add the appropriate endings to the following words:

flush____   bind____
nest ____   bank____
test ____   assist____

3.   When the rule for doubling consonants is known, adding endings to other words will be easy.

Here are some exercises for using the above rules.

a.   Add "ing" to these words:

hit ____   sip____
zip ____   fit____
drop____   stop____
hop____   dip____

b.   Add "est," "er," or "ed" to these words:

glad____   big____
sad ____   ship____
mad____   hit____
fat ____   trip____

Rule for Hard and Soft Sounds of "c"

The letter "c" confuses children because sometimes it has the sound of "k" and sometimes the sound of "s."

Write and say the words cat, cook, cute, come, cent, city, ceiling, center, cell, cab, cash, cap, cot, cedar, and cement.

Help your student write the following rules: *If "c" comes before the vowels "a," "o," or "u," it has the hard sound of a "k." However, if "c" comes before "e" or "i," it has the soft sound of "s."*

Rule for the Hard and Soft Sounds of "g"

The consonant "g" is another difficult letter for students. The letter "g" is hard in gate, go, got, game, guppy, goose. It is soft in gem, German, geography, general, gentle, and giant.

The rule for "g" is similar to the sound of "c" but there are exceptions to watch, such as girl, give, get. *If "g" comes before the vowels "a," "o," or "u," it is hard. It is soft if it comes before "e" or "i."*

Remind students that English pronunciations are not always consistent, but that it does help to know what the general rules are.

APPENDIX

ADDED MATERIALS FOR SKILLS
DEVELOPMENT BY TOPIC AND AGE LEVELS

Basic Vocabulary

THE AMERICANS ALL SERIES
Field Educational Publications
106 W. Station Street
Barrington, IL 60010

SKILLS: Reading   Series
USER: Ages 7-13   c1968

A series of high-interest books suitable for supplementary reading for slow learners at the junior high level. Each story centers around a young person of a particular racial or ethnic background during the time in history when that racial or ethnic group was effecting changes in this country. The primary aim is to guide students toward critical thinking, understanding and insight into other cultures. A teacher's manual covers all 8 titles and offers teaching suggestions.

AUTHORS: Richard E. Gross, John Rambeau and others

COMMUNICATIONS 1, 2 & 3
    Follett
    1010 W. Washington Blvd.
    Chicago, IL 60607

SKILLS: Reading Development   Series
USER: Ages 6-11   c1965

There are 3 titles in this series: GETTING STARTED (1)
for reading level 0-2; ON THE WAY (2) for reading level
3-4; and FULL SPEED AHEAD (3) for reading level 5-6.
These books utilize applied linguistics to teach writing,
spelling and basic English to adults and young adults. They
are designed to raise the non-reader to a level of functional
literacy in as short a time as possible. Reading is taught by
the "pattern" method after the student learns the alphabet.

AUTHOR: Josephine Bauer

DEEP-SEA ADVENTURE SERIES
Harr Wagner, now available from
Field Educational Publications, Inc.
106 W. Station Street
Barrington, IL 60010

SKILLS:	Reading	Series
USER:	Ages 8-17	c1959

Twelve adventure stories for readers in grades 3 through high school who are reading at 2nd and 5th grade level. A teacher's manual suggests core procedures for various situations, offers background information on deep-sea diving, and provides specific plans for skill development and evaluation.

AUTHORS: Coleman, Hewett and others

DOG STORIES IN BASIC VOCABULARY
Garrard Publishing Company
Champaign, IL 50700

SKILLS: Reading   176p.
USER: Ages 7-12   c1954

One of a series of books written at the 2nd grade level using the Dolch 220 basic sight words and 95 common nouns. Designed to promote independent reading. DOG STORIES contains 18 true stories about the intelligence and devotion displayed by different breeds of dogs.

AUTHOR: Edward Dolch

A FIRST COURSE IN PHONIC READING
Educators Publishing Service
75 Moulton Street
Cambridge, MA 02138

SKILLS: Reading Development   80p.
USER: Ages 6-10   c1965

A book written for children in 2nd and 3rd grades who haven't learned to read. Intended primarily for students with disabilities, the book may be helpful to anyone who needs a basic foundation in phonics. Both the student workbook and teacher's manual are available in later editions from the publisher.

AUTHOR: Lida G. Helson

THE JIM FOREST READERS
Field Educational Publications
106 W. Station Street
Barrington, IL 60010

SKILLS: Reading   Series
USER: Ages 9-15

Ghost towns, floods and daily activities in a big forest pre-
serve are blended with conservation concepts, suspense and
humor in these readers written at 1.7 to 3.2 reading level.
Practice books, available only from the publisher, make
this series especially appropriate for remedial use.

AUTHORS: John Rambeau, Nancy Rambeau and others

MKM READING SYSTEM
MKM
809 Kansas City Street
Rapid City, South Dakota 57701

SKILLS: Reading
USER: Ages 6-10

Kit
c1963

Originally designed to help children with learning disabilities learn to break the reading code, this revised edition is also appropriate as a foundation program beginning at the 1st grade level. The unique feature is the use of 26 mnemonic posters which present phonetic, linguistic, reading and spelling principles. Reinforcement books provide activities which stress motor and perceptual skills development for the first part of the program and then develop concepts of vowels and consonants, prefixes and suffixes, etc. Games and puzzles are also used as reinforcement material. A sample available for loan.

AUTHORS: Leland D. Michael, James W. King and others

THE MORGAN BAY MYSTERIES
Morgan Bay Mystery Series
Harr Wagner, now available from
Field Educational Publications, Inc.
106 W. Station Street
Barrington, IL 60010

SKILLS: Reading   Series
USER: Ages 9-17   c1962

High interest mystery stories written in controlled vocabulary from 2.3-4.1 reading levels. Fast-paced, suspenseful
and sometimes humorous, these stories provide motivation
for students reading below grade level. A teacher's manual
suggests effective ways to use the series in different situations and offers suggestions for introducing each book.

AUTHORS: John Rambeau and Nancy Rambeau

PACEMAKER STORY BOOKS
Fearon/Lear Siegler
6 Davis Drive
Belmont, CA 94002

SKILLS: Reading Development   Series
USER: Ages 12-17   c1963

These books for students reading below grade level are
written on approximately 2nd grade level:

      Treasure in the Ruins
      A Bomb in the Submarine
      A Gun from Nowhere
      Adventure in the Snow
      Ride on a Rainy Afternoon
      Mystery at Camp Sunshine

AUTHOR: G. R. Crosler

READING BETTER WITH JIM KING
Steck Vaughn
P.O. Box 2028
Austin, Texas 78767

SKILLS: Reading Development   136p.
USER: Ages 12-17   c1969

This book contains 40 high interest stories on a primary reading level, designed for teenagers in special education classes. The illustrated workbook has controlled vocabulary and frequent reviews and can be used with students of varied intelligence and reading levels.

AUTHOR: Ann Truitt (Lake)

READING INCENTIVE LANGUAGE PROGRAM
Bowmer - 622 Rodier Dr.
Glendale, CA 91201

SKILLS: Reading Development   Kits
USER: Ages 9-17   c1967

This program includes 16 titles, listed below, all of which are written on the third grade reading level but are of high interest and help develop independent reading and communication skills through high school. Each kit contains one filmstrip, one cassette, ten student booklets and one teacher's guide. Please specify title when ordering. Karting, Slot Car Racing, Drag Racing, Drag Racing Funny Cars, Teen Fair, Horses, Dune Buggies, Motorcycle Racing, Minibikes, VW Bugs, Snowmobiles, Bicycles, Bicycle Racing, Hot Air Balloons, Dogs, Custom Cars, Surfing, Motorcycles, Mighty Midgets, and Dune Buggy Racing.

AUTHORS: Ed and Ruth Radlauer

REMEDIAL READING DRILLS
George Wahr Publishing Company
304-1/2 So. State Street
Ann Arbor, MI 48104

SKILLS: Reading Development   Iv
USER: Ages 7-12   c1955

These drills are designed primarily to aid children who
have become retarded in reading. The exercises are likely
to be most effective in the following cases: the reading
ability is below fourth grade; the child has a severe special
reading disability; the child is educable in sound blending;
any extreme visual or auditory defects have been corrected;
the child is motivated and cooperative.

AUTHORS: Thorleif G. Hegge, Samuel A. Kirk and
            others

SIGNS
New Reader's Press
now available from
Educational Activities, Inc.
P.O. Box 392
Freeport, NY 11520

SKILLS:	Reading Development	Series
USER:	Ages 7-15	c1971, c1973

Three paperback books and a set of four filmstrips with guide are designed to provide slow, reluctant, or beginning readers with a successful reading experience. The content is a succession of signs from stores, streets, signs advertising food, etc. The books and filmstrips, which may be used together but are not dependent on each other, should interest all students in words and experiences prior to formal reading instruction. Suggestions on uses for the materials are offered in the teacher guide.

AUTHOR: Sol Gordon

SKIPPY THE SKUNK
Animal Adventure Series
Benefic Press
10300 West Roosevelt Road
Westchester, IL 60153

SKILLS: Reading   Kit
USER: Ages 7-12   c1963

A series of high interest easy-to-read books and records about animals, each providing scientific information in story form. Developed for primary grade readng interests from pre-primary to grade 4, each book also contains stimulating student questions and activities. Reading levels range from PP-1.

AUTHOR: Gene Darby

THERE'S A MONSTER IN MY READING PROGRAM
Bowmar
622 Rodier Drive
Glendale, CA 91201

SKILLS: Reading Development   Set
USER: Ages 7-12   c1973

A series of 12 adventure stories about a lovable monster
and his friends created from the child's own language. The
vocabulary was chosen from words used by children from
5-7 years old. Children respond imaginatively to stories set
within an urban environment. The teacher's guide also
makes suggestions as to how the stories can be used to
stimulate creativity in art and writing.

AUTHORS: Ellen Blance and Ann Cook

WILDLIFE ADVENTURE SERIES
Field Educational Publications
106 W. Station Street
Barrington IL 60010

SKILLS: Reading   Series
USER: Ages 7-15   c1964

Eight stories about animals of land and sea. Background information on habitats and habits provides for many enrichment activities. The teacher's manual also suggests art and writing activities reinforcement activities and includes a section on scientific concepts.

AUTHORS: Leonard and Briscoe

Comprehension
And Listening Skills

ACCENT ON LISTENING: EARLY PRIMARY
An AEP Listening Skills Program
Zerox - 600 Madison Avenue
New York, NY

SKILLS: Listening   Kits
USER: Ages 7-12

Designed to help kindergartners and first graders improve listening skills, there is one program for each of these levels. Materials include a 12" record, student books, and teacher's guide intended to develop skills in making inferences, seeing relationships, following directions, associating sound with concepts and more.

DEVELOPMENTAL READING TEXT
WORKBOOK SERIES
   Bobbs-Merrill
   4300 W. 62nd. Street
   Indianapolis, IN 46286

SKILLS: Reading Development   Series
USER: Ages 7-12   c1969

Each book is designed so that students must read a passage
and then answer questions thus developing comprehension
of words, phrases and sentences. Structural analysis is presented to promote word recognition and understanding of
word forms. Also presented is a complete program in phonetic analysis to help in word recognition. Teacher's editions are available.

AUTHORS: William H. Burton, Grace K. Kemp and
           others

HIGH WAY HOLIDAYS SERIES
Bowmar
622 Rodier Drive
Glendale, CA 91201

SKILLS:	Reading Comprehension	Series
USER:	Ages 7-12	c1973

This is a high interest controlled vocabulary reading program designed to teach basic reading and comprehension skills and also to complement any basic reading series to re-teach and reinforce basic skills. Objectives are stated for both the teacher and students to give a clear understanding of the purpose of each lesson. The materials include six storybooks, reinforcement books, listening tapes, teacher's manuals, and criterion reference tests. Please specify the level when ordering.

AUTHOR: Jo Stanchfield

LISTENING GAMES
   Teacher's Publishing Company
   Michigan Products
   1200 Keystone
   Lansing, MI 48909

SKILLS: Listening   132p.
USER: Ages 7-15   c1960

Building listening skills with instructional games. 141
games were designed to develop listening and understanding, important aspects of language arts and other curricula.
Each game is marked with appropriate grade levels for
grades 1-8.

AUTHORS: Guy Wagner, Max Hosier and others

MOTT BASIC LANGUAGE SKILLS PROGRAM
COMPREHENSION SERIES
Allied Education Council
P.O. Box 728
Galien, MI 49113

SKILLS: Reading   Series
USER: Ages 7-15   c1970

This series, the Read-Understand-Remember books 301-304 and 601-604, covers reading levels 2.7 to 7.0. High interest reading selections are designed to develop the student's understanding and retention of what he reads. The student must answer a question about a passage and make the correction before going on. Books 301-304 are designed to coordinate with skills taught in Semi-programmed Series books 1304-06. Books 601-604 of this series correspond with Semi-programmed Series 1607-1610. Book 160 Sound and Structure provides an introduction to this series.

AUTHORS: Byron E. Chapman and Louis Schulz

READING FOR MEANING
J. B. Lippincott Company
230 N. Michigan Avenue
Suite 525
Chicago, IL 60601

SKILLS: Reading   Series
USER: Ages 7-15   c1962

This is a dual-purpose program for remedial use with poor readers or for improving the speed, comprehension and vocabulary of able readers. Workbooks and teacher's guides for grades 4-0 are available for loan. Books for levels through grade 12 may be purchased from the publisher. Brief reading selections are followed by activities centering on comprehension, vocabulary, reading speed and critical or special purpose reading.

AUTHORS: John H. Coleman and Ann Jungebleit

Language Skills

ASK A CASTUS ROSE/ASK A DAFFODIL
Two Completely Phonetic Poetry Books
Heni Wenkart
4 Shady Hill Square
Cambridge, Massachusetts

SKILLS: Reading   2v.
USER: Ages 7-12   c1973

Both books contain poems written to help children practice readng by use of phonetic or linguistic principles. The
poems may also give the beginning reader a feeling for
poetry—its moods and the freedom it gives to language.

AUTHOR: Adele Seronde

CHANDLER READING PROGRAM
Chandler/Noble and Noble
1 Dag Hammarskjold Plaza
245 East 47th Street
New York, NY 10017

SKILLS: Reading   Series
USER: Ages 7-9   c1968

A multiethnic reading program for primary students that helps develop a positive self-image, teaches vital oral language skills prior to and with reading, and includes literature from around the world to provide a richer experience. Posters, film loops, workbooks and special poetry books for reading aloud are included, plus a readiness program and teacher's guide. Only the texts are available for loan. Please specify level, Readiness-Grade 3, when ordering.

AUTHORS: Lawrence W. Carrillo and Donald J. Bissett

THE CORNERSTONE READERS

Field Educational Publications
196 W. Station Street
Barrington, IL 60010

SKILLS: Reading Development
USER: Ages 7-12

Set
c1970

These readers are designed to develop reading skills of students in grades 1-6, reading at or below grade level. An orderly development of basic skills teaches word attack, vocabulary, comprehension, and study skills. Each book, in addition, provides selections to supplement science, social studies and English curriculums. Teacher's editions provide lesson plans, activities, and bibliographies. The five titles are:

Alphabet Soup	Reading Level 1
Bakers Dozen	Reading Level 2
Crackerjacks	Reading Level 2
Drumbeats	Reading Level 3
Elbowroom	Reading Level 4

AUTHOR: Henry A. Bamman

DISTAR & STRATEGY GAMES
  SRA - 259 E. Erie Street
  Chicago, IL 60611

SKILLS: Reading, Arithmetic, Language   Game
USER: Ages 7-13   c1972

The program consists of two types of games. The DISTAR
games supplement and reinforce skills taught in Levels I
and II of Distar Reading, Language and Arithmetic. Each
game can be played after a specified number of lessons in
the program. In the STRATEGY games the children learn
to make strategy decisions in order to move from the starting area to the goal. Both types of games are played on a
game board by a group of 5-7 children. When ordering
please specify whether interested in the Reading, Language
or Arithmetic game cards.

AUTHORS: Siegfried Engelmann and Doug Carnine

THE FOUNDATION PROGRAM
Open Court Correlated Language Arts Program
Open Court
Box 599
LaSalle, IL 61301

SKILLS: Pre-reading Series
USER: Ages 7-9 c1971, 1972

The Foundation Program consists of 3 workbooks and a teacher's manual. *Learning to Read and Write* is designed to teach sequential introduction to sounds, a systematic approach to blending and the development of writing skills. *Reading and Writing* continues developing these skills. The *Word Line Book* teaches blending and introduces new vocabulary.

**THE LANGUAGE ARTS BOX: 150 GAMES,
ACTIVITIES, MANIPULATIVES DESIGNED TO
MAKE LEARNING (AND TEACHING) FUN**
Creative Activity Series
        Educational Insights, Inc.
        Opportunities for Learning
        5024 Lankershim Blvd.
        North Hollywood, CA 91601

SKILLS:	Basic Language Skills	Activity Cards
USER:	Ages 9-15	c1972

An index file box filled with 4" x 6" cards, each containing an idea for strengthening written and oral communication skills. Games, poems, puzzles, and activities add interest to all basic programs.

LANGUAGE GAMES
Teacher's Publishing Corp./
Michigan Products
1200 Keystone
Lansing, MI 48909

SKILLS: Spelling, Usage   144p.
USER: Ages 9-15   c1963

A volume of instructional games designed to strengthen language skills. 150 games for all grades encourage clarity and creativity in speech, vocabulary, dictionary skills, spelling and usage.

AUTHORS: Guy Wagner, Max Hosier and others

THE READING BOX: READING GAMES AND ACTIVITIES
Creative Activity Series
    Educational Insights, Inc.
    Opportunities for Learning
    5420 Lankershim Blvd.
    North Hollywood, CA 91601

SKILLS: Reading   Activity Cards
USER: Ages 9-15   c1972

One of a series of activity cards packaged in index-file boxes and filled with ideas for projects, games, experiments, field trips and more. The reading box contains 150 teaching techniques for grades K-8, including readiness activities, comprehension and listening skill builders, phonics games, dictionary skills, all designed to make the reading process come alive.

READING FOR CONCEPTS
McGraw Hill
5940 Touhy Avenue
Niles, IL 60648

SKILLS: Reading Development   Series
USER: Ages 6-15   c1970

An 8-book series, with teacher's guide, presents light non-fiction in reading levels from 1.6 to 6.8 for remedial, corrective and developmental classes. The stories provide fundamental ideas about living to strengthen comprehension skills and increase awareness of people. Critical reading, drawing conclusions and making inferences are stressed.

AUTHOR: William Liddle

READING GAMES
Teacher's Publishing Corp./
Michigan Products
1200 Keystone Avenue
Lansing, MI 48909

SKILLS: Reading Development   128p.
USER: Ages 6-15   c1960

Educational games to strengthen reading skills. Most games can be played by individuals or groups with a teacher. Some can be used in other subject areas.

AUTHORS: Guy Wagner, Max Hosier

REMEDIAL READING WORKTEXT
Modern Curriculum Press
13900 Prospect Road
Cleveland, Ohio 41136

SKILLS: Reading   128p.
USER: Ages 7-12   c1973

The concept of the Remedial Reading Worktext is that reading skills (word-recognition, decoding and auditory discrimination) should be taught in such a way that the student can master them one at a time. The program then follows with practice in reading materials in which the vocabulary is controlled so that the vocabulary demands only those skills mastered by the student. May be used in either individualized or group instruction.

AUTHOR: Alice D. Lorenz

TRAY PUZZLE GRAMMAR
  Ideal
  Michigan Products, Inc.
  1200 Keystone Avenue
  Lansing, MI 48909

SKILLS: Phonics, Grammar   Game
USER: Ages 7-12

A set of 4 puzzles presenting homonyms, synonyms, opposites, comprehension. The puzzles are self-teaching, self-correctional and provide reinforcement materials. The good reader, poor reader, non-reader and children with motor coordination problems can benefit. Each of 4 trays contains an 8-1/2" x 11" answer board permanently attached to the bottom of the plastic tray and a set of puzzle pieces containing the words or clues on one side with part of a picture on the other. Pieces are placed over the correct answers, picture side up to complete the picture.

Vocabulary
Dictionary And Alphabet

BASIC SIGHT VOCABULARY CARDS
Garrard Publishing Company
Champaign, IL 61820

SKILLS: Vocabulary   Flashcards
USER: Ages 7-12   c1952

220 cards, 2 x 3-1/2 inches, provide practice in recognizing basic sight words. Helpful for remedial readers in identifying the vocabulary that makes up 50% to 75% of school reading matter. Good second graders and average third graders should recognize these words. An instruction sheet provides ideas for using.

AUTHOR: Edward W. Dolch

CONTEMPORARY VOCABULARY GAMES PRIMARY
Prentice Hall Learning Systems
Englewood Cliffs, N.J. 07632

SKILLS: Sight Words   96p.
USER: Ages 7-12   c1974

This book contains a compilation of games, gameboards, and activities to be used to enhance the teaching and learning of reading skills and concepts at the primary level. The materials may be used in large or small groups or as independent activities in learning centers. The words were selected from the Dolch Word List, Harrison-Jacobson Core Words for First Grade, Harper Row, and Macmillan Word List.

AUTHOR: Megan L. Senini

FUN WITH CAPITAL AND LOWERCASE LETTERS
Instructo McGraw Hill
Available from Michigan Products
1200 Keystone
Lansing, MI 48909

SKILLS: Alphabet Recognition and Sequencing   Kit
USER: Ages 7-12   c1974

An alphabet puzzle set, worksheet board, activities and a letter matching board provide practice and reinforcement in the recognition and identification of capital and lower-case letters. This supplemental kit is self-directing and self-correcting and comes with directions for teachers and a class progress chart. Perfect for a classroom learning center.

GROUP WORD TEACHING GAME
Garrard Publishing Company
Champaign, IL 61820

SKILLS: Vocabulary   Game
USER: Ages 7-12   c1944

This game, consisting of nine sets of six cards each resembling bingo cards, but with words in the squares, provides a means by which a student or a group can learn through play the 220 basic sight words. Directions for playing are included.

AUTHOR: Edward W. Dolch

LEARNING THE CONSONANT BLENDS WITH AMOS AND HIS FRIENDS
Imperial International Learning
247 W. Court Street
Kankakee, IL 60901

SKILLS:	Pre-reading	Kit
USER:	Ages 7-12	c1967

This kit is a sequel to *Learning the Alphabet and its Sounds.* The materials include a picture card that represents each of the consonant blends, duplication masters for followup activities, a cassette tape, and a teacher's manual. Each blend is introduced by a song to the tune of *"Row, Row, Row Your Boat,"* and the tape allows the children to hear how each song should be sung before trying it. "Enrichment Stories" are also suggested for some sounds.

AUTHOR: Hope S. Joyce

MY ALPHABET BOOK
   Charles E. Merrill
   1300 Alum Creek Road
   Columbus, Ohio 43216

SKILLS: Letter Recognition   61p.
USER: Ages 7-12   c1967

This paperbound booklet (8-1/2 x 11 inches) teaches various skills dealing with the alphabet and letter recognition. It can be used in teaching the alphabet itself, or as a device to teach visual discrimination, left to right progression, or basic language skills.

AUTHORS: Rosemary G. Wilson and Mildred K.
           Randolph

MY PUZZLE BOOK
  Garrard Publishing Company
  Champaign, IL 61820

SKILLS: Vocabulary
USER: Ages 7-12

2v.
c1964

Book 1 uses the easier half of the 220 Dolch Basic Sight vocabulary. Book 2 contains the other half. Each page has a list of words, sentences with blanks and empty boxes resembling crossword puzzles. The student learns by properly filling in the blanks and working the puzzles.

AUTHORS: Marguerite P. Dolch and Lillian Ostrofsky

READING GAMES AND DEVICES
  Personalized Learning Association
  P.O. Box 886
  San Jose, CA 95106

SKILLS: Reading Development   1v.
USER: Ages 7-13   c1974

This book is for teachers but the activities described here
are readily applicable to classroom use. The games and devices emphasize word attack skills, word recognition,
phrase reading and comprehension. Many are printed full-
size so that they can be copied directly in a variety of ways.
All activities are accompanied by directions for assembling
and suggestions for use.

AUTHORS: Robert J. Ramonda and John D. Morlan

SKILL DEVELOPMENT BOOKLETS
Ideas in Education
Box 323
Villa Park, IL 60181

SKILLS:	Classification, Vocabulary	12 titles
USER:	Ages 7-13	c1975

This series includes the following titles: *Rhyme Time* - provides practice in consonant substitutions, also shows rhyming words sound alike, but are not always spelled alike; *Quiz Search* - search for words from clues given; *Match Mates* - exercises on word meaning, relationship of words and matching; *Form-a-Word* - introduces word building skills; *World Power Books* - each of two contains 150 most commonly used vocabulary words; *Same-Opposites Sound Alikes* - for vocabulary development; *Alpha Track Books* - recognizing and tracking the alphabet; *Track-a-Word Books* - these provide practice for omissions, substitutions and letter and word reversals.

THORNDIKE BARNHART BEGINNING DICTIONARY
Scott Foresman
1900 East Lake Avenue
Glenview, IL 60025

SKILLS: Spelling   768p.
USER: Ages 7-13   c1972

A dictionary designed for use in grades 3 and 4. There is a
section on how to use the dictionary preceding the entries,
which consist of simple definitions. Illustrations for some
of the terms appear in the margins.

AUTHORS: E. L. Thorndike and Clarence L. Barnhart

USING YOUR DICTIONARY
John C. Winston Company
Philadelphia, PA

SKILLS: Spelling   80p.
USER: Ages 7-13   c1958

Exercises in alphabetizing, spelling, choosing correct definitions and pronunciation, using the appendix, and finding
appropriate illustrations are presented here in increasingly
complex steps.

AUTHORS: Isabelle F. Forst, George Goldberg et. at.

WORD BANK
Mott Basic Language Skills Program
    Allied Education Council
    P. O. Box 78
    Galien, MI

SKILLS: Vocabulary   177p.
USER: Ages 7-15   c1969

Written on reading levels 3.0 - 5.0 each word is identified
by a photograph of the object. The word is also used in the
context of the sentence and as a review for each unit; the
student must read and comprehend a short selection in
which unit words are incorporated.

AUTHORS: Byron E. Chapman and Louis Schulz

WORD STUDY FOR IMPROVED READING
  Globe Book Company
  175 Fifth Avenue
  New York, NY 10010

SKILLS:	Reading	100p.
USER:	Ages 13-	c1970

A workbook whose purpose is remediation of the skills needed for reading, spelling, vocabulary and the use of words in sentences. Each section contains "Things to do for Practice" which the teacher will need to check and which provide the necessary drill for recall. The book can be used from junior high on.

AUTHOR: A. Allen Robbins

WORKING WITH THE ALPHABET ACTIVITY CARDS
Prentice Hall Learning Systems
Englewood Cliffs, N.J. 07632

SKILLS:	Alphabetizing, Letter Recognition	Act. Cards
USER:	Ages 7-12	c1975

This set of 49 self-directing cards provides activities for a wide range of grades and ability levels. They may be used for introduction, reinforcement, practice, or enrichment. Most of these exercises consist of putting words in alphabetical order.

Phonics And Spelling

BEGINNING SOUNDS, LEVELS 1 AND 2
Reading Readiness Series
Continental Press
P. O. Box 554
Elgin, IL 60120

SKILLS: Phonics   Duplicating Masters
USER: Ages 7-12   c1966

Nonreading activities in phonics, suitable for use in special classes. Lessons provide practice in identifying and discriminating initial sounds. A teacher's guide is included with each set.

AUTHOR: Ethel S. Maney

BUILD IT - SERIES I, II, III, IV
Remedial Education Press
Kingsbury Center
2138 Bancroft Place, N.W.
Washington, D.C. 20008

SKILLS: Phonics   Game
USER: Ages 7-15   c1967

A phonetic game without pictures for primary grades that could also be used with older students. Deck I helps in teaching single consonants and short vowels. Deck II teaches consonant blends and short vowels. Deck III helps teach single consonants and long vowel combinations. Deck IV helps in teaching the consonant blends with the long vowel combinations. Instructions for playing are included with each deck, all of which may be previewed separately.

AUTHOR: Jean White

COMPLETELY PHONETIC STORY BOOKS
Heni Wenkart Publishing
4 Shady Hill Square
Cambridge, MA 02138

SKILLS:	Reading, Spelling	Series
USER:	Ages 7-9	c1970

A series of beginning readers that, instead of being limited in vocabulary, are made up of words which are completely phonetic. The student need know only a couple of vowel sounds and sounds of the consonants to read a whole book. And by introducing one new vowel sound at a time, the student can read each succeeding book. Gaily illustrated, these paperbacks may provide many slow readers with a successful experience.

AUTHOR: Henny Wenkart

CONSONANTS FLOOR PUZZLE
Trend Enterprises/R. H. Stone, Dist.
13735 Puritan
Detroit, MI 48227

SKILLS: Consonants, Vocabulary   Game
USER: Ages 7-12   c1974

This 27" x 39" self-correcting floor puzzle has 50 pieces in all. Ten large base pieces make up the panoramic urban background. Twenty removable pieces feature initial consonant letters; the remaining twenty pieces contain illustrations representing each initial consonant's sound. Instructions are included.

CONTINUOUS PROGRESS IN SPELLING
INTERMEDIATE
Economy - 1901 N. Walnut
Oklahoma City, OK 73105

SKILLS: Spelling, Vocabulary   Kit
USER: Ages 9-15   c1972

This is an individualized spelling program which permits each student to study at his own level and progress at his own rate. A student studies only the words he does not know. Each student discovers, from organized word lists geared to his own level, those words he cannot spell. Words are arranged sequentially through the 16 levels according to frequency of use and difficulty. Within the first 12 levels, the words are grouped by phonic, structural, and modified linguistic generalization. The teacher's guide tells you this and more.

AUTHORS: Edwin A. Read, Ruel A. Allred and others

FORM-A-SOUND PHONIC CARDS
Ideal - Michigan Products
1200 Keystone
Lansing, MI 48909

SKILLS: Phonics   Act. Cards
USER: Ages 7-12   c1972

These phonic cards were developed to instruct children in
a basic foundation of phonetics. In kindergarten they can
be used for language development and pre-reading exercises; in primary grades, these can be used in reading and
spelling programs. A card is provided for each consonant
and vowel sound. Along with the letter presentation of the
sound, each card has a picture of the oral cavity making
the sound in isolation, a stop light indicating whether the
speech motor is off or on, and a picture of the speech partner if the sound has a speech partner. Suggested uses and
instructions are included.

AUTHOR: Edward L. Kelley

GINN WORD ENRICHMENT PROGRAM
Ginn and Company
450 West Algonquin Avenue
Arlington Heights, IL 60005

SKILLS: Spelling   Series
USER: Ages 7-12   c1968, c1974

Designed to provide children in grades 1-6 with structured learning experiences that will enable them to master skills and abilities in word analysis. Students will also increase speaking and reading vocabularies. This independent word study program can be used with any reading series while developing word-analysis skills more quickly than the basal texts. Can be used with middle and upper grade pupils needing remediation.

AUTHORS: Theodore Clymer and Thomas C. Barrett

THE GO FISH SOUND GAME, SERIES I AND II
Remedial Education Press
Kingsbury Center
2138 Bancroft Place, N.W.
Washington, D.C. 20008

SKILLS:	Consonant Sounds	Game
USER:	Ages 7-15	c1968

Both of these are card games used to teach consonant sounds (Series I) and consonant blends (Series II). For each initial consonant and consonant blend, there is a picture of an object beginning with that sound. The word is also spelled out. Rules for playing are included.

AUTHOR: Marion Kingsbury

LETTER CARDS (Large Type)
    Ideal - Michigan Products
    1200 Keystone
    Lansing, MI 48909

SKILLS: Letter Identification, Spelling   Act. Cards
USER: Ages 7-12

This box contains an assortment of upper and lower case letters printed on 1" square card stock. Some of the lower case letters are smaller; some punctuation marks are also included. Students could use these to practice motor coordination, spelling and letter recognition. Teachers could make up a variety of games for students to play. There are no instructions—only lots of tiny pieces.

LETTER-PICTURE SOLITAIRE
(Houghton Mifflin Reading Program)
    Houghton Mifflin
    1900 S. Batavia
    Geneva, IL 60134

SKILLS: Phonics   Flashcards
USER: Ages 7-12   c1972

In a game-like setting, beginning consonant-sound associa-
tions are reinforced. The game has two sets of 88 picture
cards and 22 letter cards (for 18 consonants and 4 speech
consonants), and two ring binders. Cards are stacked on
posts in the ring binder. On the first post are letter cards;
the other four posts contain picture cards. Each of the
four picture-card stacks shows an object that begins with
the sound represented by the exposed letter in the first
stack. Self-checking is possible.

AUTHOR: James D. Garzelloni

THE MCP BASIC PHONICS PROGRAM
Modern Curriculum Press
13900 Prospect Road
Cleveland, OH 44136

SKILLS: Phonics   Series
USER: Ages 7-12   c1971

Text, workbook and teacher manual on each of three levels, grades 1-3. The series features auditory discrimination, phonetic skills in the order of their linguistic importance, and provides adequate maintenance and reinforcement through the workbook exercises.

AUTHORS: Elwell, Murray and others

MY WORD-CLUE DICTIONARY
Macmillan Company
539 Turtle Creek South Drive
Indianapolis, IN 46227

| SKILLS: | Spelling, Usage | 309p. |
| USER: | Ages 7-12 | c1967 |

This beginning dictionary contains all words introduced in the 2nd grade of Macmillan Reading Program. In addition, it also lists many variant forms of the words that are not actually used in the readers. The student may ultimately be able to use this book independently to prepare for reading lessons. Helps on how to use the dictionary are included.

AUTHORS: Albert J. Harris and Mae Knight Clark

PHONICS WE USE
Lyons and Carnahan/Meredity Corp.
39 South LaSalle Street
Chicago, IL 60616

SKILLS: Phonics   Series
USER: Ages 7-12   c1964

A series of workbooks teaching or reviewing phonics and
other word-recognition skills. Book A can be used with
pre-primer or primer level students. Book B with 1st reader
level, etc. Book F is intended for 5th year students and
provides a refresher course for students beyond the 5th
year who need help with independent attack on words.

AUTHORS: Mary Meighten, Marjorie Pratt and others

PHONETICS FACTORY
Ideal - Michigan Products
1200 Keystone
Lansing, MI 48909

SKILLS: Phonics   Kit
USER: Ages 7-12   c1973

This is an auditory-visual program developed to instruct
children in a basic foundation of phonics. The program
contains six cassettes with thirty-four recorded lessons and
accompanying spirit master worksheets. There is a recorded lesson and worksheet for each consonant sound, long
vowel sound, short vowel and digraph sound. The auditory
portion explains how to make the sounds in isolation and
provides practice in auditory feedback and discriminating
sounds as they are used in words. Instructions are included.

AUTHOR: Edward L. Kelley

**PHONETIC WORD CARDS AND REMEDIAL
TRAINING FOR CHILDREN WITH SPECIFIC
DISABILITY IN READING, SPELLING AND
PENMANSHIP**
The Gillingham Manual, 7th ed.
    Educators Publishing Service, Inc.
    75 Moulton Street
    Cambridge, MA 02138

SKILLS: Phonics, Reading, etc.   344p.
USER: Ages 7-12   c1960

This manual and accompanying word cards provide the
basics of the Gillingham method of teaching reading to students with specific language disability. The same method,
with some modification, may be used to prevent reading
disabilities and to teach adult illiterates. The technique is a
simple approach to phonics. First the sounds of letters are
taught, then built into words. This is based on the association of visual, auditory and kinesthetic elements. The word
cards contain simple words, syllabified words, and detach-
ed syllables.

AUTHORS: Anna Gillingham and Bessie W. Stillman

PHONICS FLASH CARDS/BEGINNERS
Ed-u-cards
Available from Michigan Products
1200 Keystone Avenue
Lansing, MI 48910

SKILLS: Phonics   Kit/Game
USER: Ages 7-12   c1966

Thirty-six cards, regular playing card size, in a plastic box provide drill in letter recognition and basic phonics for beginning readers.

PHONICS PICTURE CARDS
Modern Curriculum Press
13900 Prospect Road
Cleveland, OH 44136

SK LLS: Phonics   Flashcards
US R: Ages 7-15

This box contains 176 picture cards, 5" x 8-1/2", depicting objects that are familiar to children in the first grade. The cards are numbered and grouped in various categories to best assist the teacher in the specific phonics skill being presented. Words are grouped by beginning consonant, short vowel, long vowel, consonant blend and consonant digraph. These cards are designed to be used with MCP Phonics Program and the Phonics Is Fun Program, but would be a useful supplement to any phonics program.

PLAY WITH A AND T
   Child's World
   Box 681
   Elgin, IL 60120

SKILLS: Basic Spelling,   Unpaged
           Letter Recognition
USER: Ages 7-12   c1973

One of a series of alphabet books, each of which takes a
vowel and adds consonants to make familiar 3 and 4 letter
words. In this supplemental reading book, little "a" and
"t" join other letter people to make "cat," "rat" and
"mat."

AUTHOR: Jane Belk Moncure

READING SKILLS: A PHONICS APPROACH
McGraw-Hill
Princeton Road
Hightstown, N.J. 08520

SKILLS: Reading Development   Series
USER: Ages 7-12   c1975

The core of this program consists of six pupil's books, a teacher's guide, a set of Answer Sticks which serve to alternately conceal and reflect the mirror-image answers. Each book serves a reading purpose and reviews all concepts presented in previous books of the series. The series is compatible with any reading series and provides instruction in phonics, structural analysis, sight-word recognition, use of context clues and grammatical structure.

AUTHOR: Louise Binder Scott

READING WITH PHONICS
   J. B. Lippincott
   230 N. Michigan
   Suite 525
   Chicago, IL 60601

SKILLS: Phonics, Reading   128p.
USER: Ages 7-12   c1967

A primary level reader that uses the phonics approach to
teaching reading. Emphasizes one sound at a time and the
book is illustrated in color. At the end of each section,
there is a review of words just taught.

AUTHORS: Julie Hay, Charles E. Wingo and others

SHORT SHORTS

The Remedial Education Press
Kingsbury Center
2138 Bancroft Place, N.W.
Washington D.C. 20008

SKILLS: Phonic Analysis   Game
USER: Ages 7-12   c1967, c1969

This is a word building game designed to help in teaching the first steps in phonetic analysis. The game uses three simple sounds for each word: initial consonant, short vowel and final consonant. Two, three or four persons can play; the object is to form as many words as possible while taking turns. Instructions for playing are included.

AUTHOR: Margaret Suter Rood

SHORT VOWEL DRILL
   The Remedial Education Press
   Kingsbury Center
   2138 Bancroft Place, N.W.
   Washington, D.C. 20008

SKILLS: Short Vowel Sounds   Game
USER: Ages 7-15   c1944

These cards can be used to teach short vowel sounds in
both reading and spelling. The sounds are taught here
through association with pictures beginning with these
sounds. Instructions are included.

AUTHOR: Marion Kingsbury

SILLY SOUNDS GAME OF INITIAL CONSONANTS

Ideal - Michigan Products, Inc.
1200 Keystone Avenue
Lansing, MI 48909

SKILLS: Phonics   Game
USER: Ages 7-12

A game designed to teach consonants and provide practice in developing vocabulary. It consists of playing board, spinner, advance-penalty cards and tokens. Two to six players may participate. Instructions for playing are printed on box lid along with suggestions for variations.

SNOOPY'S YELLOW CODE BOOK
Holt Rinehart
645 N. Michigan Avenue
Chicago, IL 60611

SKILLS: Phonics   64p.
USER: Ages 7-12   c1972

After an alphabet review, vowels and consonants are introduced by *Peanuts* characters. All of Snoopy's code books
present phonics skills in sequential order, as they are introduced in many basal texts. Most of the skills taught in this
title are presented through pictures so students who have
not mastered sight words can still benefit.

AUTHORS: Charles Schulz and Kathryn M. Lumley

SOUNDS FOR YOUNG READERS, VOL. II
Kimbo
Box 246
Deal, N.J. 07723

SKILLS: Phonics   Record
USER: Ages 7-12

This 33-1/3 rpm record systematically introduces the beginning phonetic elements necessary to all well integrated reading programs. The program is divided into four parts: initial consonants, initial consonant blends, terminal consonants and medial vowels. The record can be used at the kindergarten level with mature children but will be more effective at the first, second or third grade levels. It should also be of value to children with specific audio and speech differential problems. A teacher's guide provides followup activities.

SOUNDS FOR YOUNG READERS, VOL. III
  Kimbo
  Box 246
  Deal, N.J. 07723

SKILLS: Phonics   Record
USER: Ages 7-12

This 33-1/3 rpm record introduces children to vowel and
consonant letters. It aids in the teaching of the long and
short sounds of a,e,i,o,u. Four general rules of pronunciation to guide children in word perception are also introduced. The record may be used by individual or by the entire class. Most of the exercises are self-correcting. A teacher's guide provides preparation and followup activities.

SOUNDS FOR YOUNG READERS, VOL. IV
Kimbo
Box 246
Deal, N.J. 07723

SKILLS: Phonics   Record
USER: Ages 7-12

This 33-1/3 rpm record is designed to aid the child's understanding of difficult consonant sounds. It also helps the
child to sharpen and develop his word analysis skills. Especially suited to grades two through four, this record will
also prove valuable to the child with specific phonetic difficulties at any grade level. A teacher's guide provides
introduction to the lessons and followup activities.

SOUNDS FOR YOUNG READERS, VOL. V
   Kimbo
   Box 246
   Deal, N.J. 07723

SKILLS: Grammar   Record
USER: Ages 7-12

This 33-1/3 rpm record introduces and develops word
attack and analysis skills necessary for intermediate grades.
Subjects included are syllabication, accenting, root words,
word endings and compound words. The record begins
with a review of the alphabet and progresses to a discussion of vowel and consonant usage. Pupil participation is
stressed. A teacher's guide provides general directions and
followup activities.

SOUNDS FOR YOUNG READERS, VOL. VI
Kimbo
Box 246
Deal, N.J. 07723

SKILLS: Phonics   Record
USER: Ages 7-12

This 33-1/3 rpm record introduces vowel analysis skills necessary for the intermediate grades. The general understanding of the variability of vowel pronunciation and spelling is promoted through the use of contextual clues, silent letters, vowel modifiers, and the identification and pronunciation of diphthongs. A teacher's guide provides introductions to the lessons as well as followup activities.

VOWEL DOMINOES
   The Remedial Education Press
   Kingsbury Center
   2138 Bancroft Place, N.W.
   Washington, D.C. 20008

SKILLS: Short Vowel Sounds   Game
USER: Ages 7-12   c1941

This game teaches students short vowel sounds and can be used as a drill even after the student has some knowledge of vowels. Intended for children in second grade and beyond, the value of the game lies in the child seeing the letter, identifying the short vowel sound to himself and then finding a picture which contains that sound. Instructions for playing are included.

AUTHOR: Marion Kingsbury

INDEX

NOTES

NOTES

NOTES

NOTES

NOTES

NOTES

Books From
THE SCHOOL AIDES SERIES

THE READING TUTOR'S HANDBOOK: GRADES 2-6 by Ruth Evelyn Rogers, Edsel L. Erickson and Ruth Burkett Park. This is an easily read handbook designed primarily for tutors to assist teachers in schools or in private practice. Major areas: 1) a general introduction to tutoring; school procedures and ethical requirements, conferences with teachers, meeting with students, and individual differences; 2) requirements and resources for conducting private tutoring services; 3) procedures for assessing reading problems; 4) activities to develop specific reading skills in a tutoring situation; and 5) annotated listing of added materials for skills development. (Hardback, ISBN 0-918452-00-7, $11.95; Paperback, ISBN 0-918452-01-5, $8.95)

READING ASSESSMENT BOOKLET: GRADES 2-6. This record booklet includes pre-tutoring tests covering pre-primer through sixth grade levels of silent and oral reading skills. Instructions are provided, along with forms, for presenting results to teachers or parents. (Paperback, ISBN 0-918452-02-3, per copy: $.75; pkgs. of 10: $4.50)

STUDENT'S READING TEST BOOK: GRADES 2-6. This booklet is for use with the above **READING ASSESSMENT BOOKLET: GRADES 2-6.** Included are a series of stories graded from pre-primer through the sixth grade level. (Paperback, ISBN 0-918452-03-1, per copy: $1.95; pkgs. of 5: $7.50)

THE SCHOOL VOLUNTEER'S HANDBOOK by Mary Veele. School administrators will want to give every lay volunteer who works in their school a copy of this handbook. It provides an excellent, easily understood discussion of the significance of volunteers; the importance of working with the school team, following school policies and ethical imperatives; and suggestions for meeting and working with students and staff. (Paperback, ISBN 0-918452-05-8, per copy: $1.45; pkgs. of 10: $6.00)

CHILDREN WITH READING PROBLEMS: A GUIDEBOOK FOR PARENTS by Ruth Erickson and Edsel L. Erickson. Parents of children with reading problems need professional guidance if they are going to assist teachers in developing their child's reading skills. This book helps teachers give parents that guidance in an easily read, step-by-step presentation of the leading causes of reading problems; the do's and don'ts of home teaching that parents need to know to support teachers; instructions for checking reading skills at home; how parents may select appropriate reading materials; and supportive home exercises. (Paperback, ISBN 0-918452-04-X, $5.95)

(see order form on reverse side)

ORDER FORM
FOR
THE SCHOOL AIDES SERIES

TO: **LEARNING PUBLICATIONS, INC.**
Box 1326 - Dept. T-26
Holmes Beach, Florida 33509

TITLES:		No. Ordered	Amount
THE READING TUTOR'S HANDBOOK: GRADES 2-6			
(Hardback)	$11.95*	_____	_____
(Paperback)	$ 8.95*	_____	_____
READING ASSESSMENT BOOKLET: GRADES 2-6	$ .75	_____	_____
(Packages of 10)	$ 4.50	_____	_____
STUDENT'S READING TEST BOOK: GRADES 2-6	$ 1.95	_____	_____
(Packages of 5)	$ 7.50	_____	_____
THE SCHOOL VOLUNTEER'S HANDBOOK	$ 1.45	_____	_____
(Packages of 10)	$ 6.00	_____	_____
CHILDREN WITH READING PROBLEMS:			
A GUIDEBOOK FOR PARENTS	$ 5.95*	_____	_____

Total _____
Florida residents add 4% sales tax _____
Please add 10% for postage/handling _____
TOTAL _____

Please send me the books I have indicated above. I am enclosing $ _____ . (U.S. dollars only in check or money order. No C.O.D.s or currency. Orders must be pre-paid unless on official, numbered order. All orders may be returned if not damaged within fifteen days for refund of purchase price minus 20% for postage and handling.)

Name_____ Street_____

City_____ State_____ Zip Code_____

*10% discount on orders of 10-19 books
 20% discount on orders of 20 or more books

(see book descriptions on reverse side)